I0225267

MORE THAN A RIB

*A Woman's Inspiration for Perspective,
Healing, and Empowerment*

A Movement and Reference Tool for

Today's Evolving Woman

RICKIE CHAFFOLD AND VARION HOWARD

MORE THAN A RIB

*A Woman's Inspiration for Perspective, Healing, and
Empowerment*

Copyright © 2013 RICKIE CHAFFOLD AND VARION HOWARD

ISBN 9780-578-12597-8

ALL RIGHTS RESERVED.

No part of this publication may be reproduced, stored in a retrieval
system, or transmitted in any form or by any means, electronic,
mechanical, photocopying, recording or otherwise without written
permission of the publisher or author.

More Than a Rib is not for everyone. We strongly feel that if you do not relate that you know someone you can share this information with who has been directly or indirectly affected by rape, divorce, single parent households, and domestic violence. The ramifications of ignoring the pain and trauma can set one up for a life of regrets and unhappiness. More Than A Rib is many things but most importantly it is a bridge over troubled waters to resources and best practices.

TO:

_____

FROM:

_____

Acknowledgements

I asked Him to keep me safe from my enemies and I started losing friends who I thought had my interest. Confused then and knowing better now, all I can do is say God is good and thank you for your traveling grace on this journey. You are a continual reminder that no weapons formed against me shall prosper. I thank you for keeping me as I continue to grow in faith and spirituality.

I also asked God to place people in my life who would embrace this project as if it were their own. People have come and gone but the one person he wanted to finish this testament is still here: me. He did not allow this for what then I thought would be a blessing because of the accountability factor. While one can be the loneliest number, one can also have structure, focus, and determination. I understand now it was for my best interest as it was a learning curve in positioning.

To Bridgett, I would not have started this journey without you … thank you.

To our families, thank you for your enduring support. It's good to have a support system that you can depend on when the glass seems half empty @ **Gloria Chaffold, Prentice Rosalyn Howard, Kemberley Chaffold, Ashunti Morris, Rickala Chaffold, Varion D. Howard II, Noah Chaffold, Nija Teal, Dayne Reliford.**

To our friends, thank you for being the comic relief in times when we thought this would never materialize. Your optimism has been the fuel to keep us going.

To our fans, thank you for the continued support over the good years and the bad years. Your loyalty is a true indicator that we have chosen the right path.

To the contributors, a special appreciation goes out to you for sharing and enabling us to reinforce the pillars with real stories of substance, consequence, and reward. The stories allow us to be personable as we tap into the real lives of your characters. Thank you.

To our church families, Pastor Rudy and Juanita Rasmus, Windsor Village, and Fountain of Praise thank you for your support.

To other friends, the movement and book would have not come to fruition without your help:

Karin Booker Dancy: Editing, ProofWhiz.com

Jennise Beverly: Dedicated visionary

Bobby D Lloyd: Graphic Artist

Athena Halton: Loyal and Devoted Friend

St. John's Church Downtown

Thecia Jenkins (Bridge Over Troubled Waters)

Dr. Carlin Barnes

Dr. Conte Terrell (Fresh Spirit)

Richard Toney (RT Counseling Service)

Amber David (City of Houston)

Ashley and Sharon Cheatham (INV Professional

Matchmakers) Houston Food Bank Outreach

Houston American Diabetes Foundation Outreach

TWEC Outreach

Harris County Health District Outreach

MD Anderson Outreach

Lisa Bogany Work Force Solution Outreach

Department of Veteran Affairs Outreach

Dr. Sedric Smith, MD

Derrick Banes I Brand Consulting

Derrick Below DB Unlimited Videography

We humbly apologize if we looked over anyone.

Dedication

There is one thing we can never get back once it is gone: Time.

We must stop wasting time and do something productive and meaningful to change ourselves. We look in the mirror day in and day out at a stranger. It is time to recognize your potential and realize your worth. It time to forgive and be free. This book is dedicated to all the women who have imprisoned themselves in half-truths, un-forgiveness, irrational decisions, and pity parties. This book is a resource that can be the first step of many, the redirection of a path, or the ending of a journey. They key is knowing who you are, what your worth is, where you are going and how you plan to get there. We hope you will benefit from this small token of our appreciation of your worth.

Be blessed in your understanding

Contents

Preface

It is evident that we have evolved as a society. Modern women of today are on a mission to maximize personal happiness through a process of self-discovery. *More Than A Rib* is a life changing resource of structure based on 9 pillars to manage day-to-day obstacles as they relate to rational decision making.

Within these 9 pillars is a collection of gut-wrenching poems and short stories from women just like you, sharing their experiences of how they have managed or not managed their emotional demons. This book is designed to enlighten, encourage and motivate you to be happy with the life you have been blessed with and to inspire you to grow beyond your immediate circumstance. *More Than A Rib* will offer you a more positive outlook on how to balance family, career, your social life and other aspects of your life. You will hear the voices of many women brave enough to share their experiences – perhaps some of their stories will be familiar to you, similar to some of your own experiences. The stories shared are evidence that you are not alone: Others have experienced your struggles but, with perseverance and determination, the battle can be won. Before you decide to abandon your vision or settle for an insignificant one, we want to encourage you to make changes in your life to harvest and achieve your goal. *More Than A Rib* will leave you with the confidence to overcome minor setback and prepare you for a major comeback.

Each pillar will discuss a particular aspect that embraces direct self-improvement and indirect relationship improvement. The only way to benefit from the pillars is to first admit that there is need for improvement. The mentality is flexible. You can address the opportunity or opportunities that have priority in your life. Listed below is a brief description of the 9 Pillars of Success.

The *More Than a Rib* lifestyle is a revolution of self-based on:

- Confronting and addressing destructive behavior
- Non emotional and rational decision making
- Accepting self-accountability and consequences
- Providing preventative measures and methods
- Introducing and reinforcing positive behavior

The 9 Pillars

- Self-Assessment
- Self-Accountability
- Self-Recovery
- Forgiveness
- Self-Renewal
- Stewardship
- Staying the Course
- Giving Back
- Commitment

Mission

This mission encompasses looking in the mirror and discovering or rediscovering "What is your Worth"?

Renewing, Recharging, and Rebuilding of one's thinking process (management of thought and emotion).

Change depreciation into appreciation.

Change how others portray women and how women portray themselves.

Facilitate reasonable and relatable best practices and resources that influence self-accountability, self-love, and self-respect.

Permissions

RAINN. (2013). Retrieved from http://www.rainn.org/get-information

Domestic Violence Facts. (2013). Retrieved from http://www.ncadv.org/files/DomesticViolenceFactSheet(National).pdf

Grall, T. (2011, December). Custodial Mothers and Fathers and Their Child Support: 2009, U.S. Census Bureau, P60-240, pg 13

Krell, R. (1972, November). Problems of the single-parent family unit. Canadian Medical Association Journal, 107(9), pgs.867-872.

Http://www.mdrc.org/publication/effects-marriage-and-divorce-families-and-children. (2004, May). MDRC, Testimony, 1-11. Retrieved from http://www.mdrc.org/publication/effects-marriage-and-divorce-families-and-children

Part I

Diagnosing the Roots and not the Symptoms

Stand Up

I was on the back row, back pew, bottom of the barrel,

End of my rope, filthy, looking for the soap, guilty,

Gluttonous, addiction at its ugliest,

Couldn't manage to pump my brakes, but I knew I was tired and had enough of it,

Lust, lies and gossip, whatever you want, I know where they got it

Sex, drugs, streets & money – I seem to lean toward those topics

I can speak on shiny wheels, diamonds & grills, poppin' pills, chiefin' kill

Even the late night hype, after hours strip club thrills, oh it's real,

But I really feel a lot of times, something is wrong,

Certain things don't sit right in my soul and inside of me something's going on

I can't take some of these preachers serious; I swear I see demons in their spirit,

And spiritually, instead of taking me where I need to be,

They're just talking too loud and taking it too far

I'm trying to find salvation, and Jesus & Satan in my head having a tug of war

Yeah, he's preaching the sermon, he has said a lot, but ain't said enough

To get me to do something so simple as just STAND UP

You know what I'm talking about, when you want to lift your hands high to praise

But this is as far as they will go

When you want to get out of your seat to go and join church & something keeps   telling you no

I don't know why it seems so hard, yeah it's awkward, but it's odd,

Some of us will get up in the middle of the night to drive across town for sex

But can't take a couple of steps for God

You better STAND UP

You drop $5, $10, $20 or more to get high,

Complain about being broke, but let the offering plate pass you by

Drop a couple of prayers here and there, just to get by

You're under attack, in the back can't get ahead and you wonder why

You think if you STAND UP, it's incriminating, it's an automatic confession

But you're worried about what the congregation thinks

So you sit in the back and miss your blessings

But, simply put, you can't worry about everyone else,

Come get a one-on-one with God for yourself and STAND UP

Then we call ourselves men, but when it's time to man up

He's just talk, he ain't man enough to do something so simple as just
STAND UP
So if you call yourselves men, then man, I'm calling you out
Because this man shall let no man stand between me and the blessings
God has for my house
STAND UP
Sister, did you ever consider?
Mister might not be well liked by your family & your crew
But mister might not be acting right because mister ain't Mr. Right for you
But how could he be right for you, when it seems that all you do
Is move through dudes and relationships based on the approval of your crew?
And since your girls said he was cute, you slept with him when you knew he didn't care
But if you're tired of waking up the next morning and finding yourself there
STAND UP for your integrity and look at the situation objectively,
Examine the role you played and stop letting these clowns treat you so disrespectfully,
And if you're tired of being there, if you've truly had enough
All you have to do right now is STAND UP

If it seems like

The weight of the world is on your shoulders because you're drowning in debt,

If it ain't one thing it's another and you're living check to check,

Scared to answer your phone, bill collectors breathing down your neck

Headache, chest pains, sleepless nights, all related to stress,

But it would be easier for you to breathe, if you weren't so easily influenced by greed

He'd open up a window and pour out a blessing there wouldn't be room to receive

Instead of asking God for something every time you hit your knees

Why don't you try giving Him thanks for giving you everything you need?

Honestly, God has already given us more than enough

Some of us can't count our blessings and acting like we're too good to STAND UP

Don't envy mine, don't envy my shine, I guarantee you I'm far from perfect

But the reason that I shine is because I'm standing in line with my purpose

God put me here to do a service and it's because I'm in that divine alignment

Instead of keeping up with the Joneses, I'm trying to stay on top of my assignment

Everybody has a part to play, everybody has a role

So why would I want what someone else has, everything that glitters ain't gold

What's for me is for me and what's for you is for you

Funny how we want what someone else has,

But don't want to go through what they had to go through,

Might not be able to handle what they had to go through,

That's why what they have is out of our reach,

But if you want what God has for you, come to your feet right now and STAND UP

When God doesn't answer our prayers immediately, we have the nerve to get mad

We ask for million dollar blessings, but won't give up our trash

So we get stuck in that situation, the situation stays the same,

We become stagnant in that madness and we begin to place blame

So we get mad at our family, mad at our girl, mad at our crew, mad at the world

Mad enough to curse, mad enough to scream, mad enough to cry, mad enough to swing

Some of us forget what we're mad about, and what we're mad about isn't worth it

Then we hurt the people we love the most, and they don't deserve it

But if you're tired of apologizing to loved ones and giving your temper control

Give God your mind, body and soul right now and STAND UP

Some of us can't ask for help, too proud and dependent on self

So egotistical we believe we don't need anyone else

And when it comes to arrogance and conceit, some of us wrote the book

Afraid to give God praise, too concerned about how we look

But that's when confidence becomes contorted and vision becomes distorted

You're so busy trying to be the center of attention you lose sight of what's important

But it's not about your clothes and it's not about your face

Because nothing is more beautiful than God's amazing grace

And that's as real as I can spit, that's as real as it's going to get

And you can't expect change if you stay where you sit

You see, we give God nothing, but we want everything

But until you put God in your endeavors, your endeavors will never change

And that's 1, 2, 3, 4, 5, 6, 7 deadly sins and I'm done

DOORS OF THE CHURCH ARE OPEN – NOW COME

Se7eN

There are no generic solutions for the insanity that people live through on an everyday basis. Everyone's madness is a case-by-case scenario. For example, there may be two identical cases of infidelity and you can guarantee that each case will be handled differently. People have different investments, different mentalities, and different values. What works for some may not work for others. What seems obvious to the rational eye may seem blurry to the irrational eye. For example, many women in relationships of domestic violence stay in these traumatizing relationships. The obvious thing would be to leave, but for reasons that cannot be understood by what we would call the "rational mind," some women stay.

I have been asked, "Why More Than A Rib?" Simple: More Than A Rib comes from the Bible story of how Eve was created out of one of Adam's ribs – but, more importantly, it represents what Eve was meant to be.

"So The Lord God caused the man to fall into a deep sleep; and while he was sleeping, He took one of the man's ribs [also translated took part of the man's side] and closed up the place with flesh. Then the Lord God made a woman from the rib He had taken out of the man, and He brought her to the man. The man said, 'This is now bone of my bones and flesh of my flesh; she shall be called woman, for she was taken out of man.' For this reason a man will leave his father and mother and be united to his wife, and they will become one flesh."

As I experience life, I see women as More Than A Rib because women are the vessels to life. Do you not think it a prophetic plan of wisdom that God made woman from man, yet gave an amazing responsibility of birth to the woman?

The power to bear, nourish, and provide for the children and the man.

The voice of reason when maturity is upon her bosom.

The one who endures more physical, mental, emotional, and spiritual pain than was meant for one person to process.

Women are undeniably the resilient heartbeat of the earth. I think it is as simple as that. Everyone has their role, but there is nowhere in the Bible where God says or illustrates that women will not evolve to and from More Than A Rib.

It Starts With Me

Luke 12:48 states: "But he who did not know, yet committed things deserving of stripes, shall be beaten with few. For everyone to whom much is given, from him much will be required; and to whom much has been committed, of him they will ask the more."

God has entrusted us with the gift of being a vessel to give life. The accountability of much being required when much is received will always be true. Women have been the rib and, more so, the backbone of societies across the globe.

Over the years, women have allowed their titles, worth, and value to depreciate as opposed to appreciate over time. A woman's worth has become cliché. The individual and collective value of being a mother, daughter, wife, sister, homemaker, and monetary provider is diminishing at an alarming rate.

The mission of the *More Than a Rib* movement is to advance a deeper and growing appreciation for women. The mission is to change how women are portrayed and how we portray ourselves. The mission is to take the seed of "Yes We Can" and apply it to continuously renew, recharge, and rebuild our thoughts and action processes.

The *More Than a Rib* movement is the facilitation of cognitive and lifestyle changes and skills. The mission is to embrace and love oneself, practice accountability, and cultivate self-respect.

Change

There are three initial steps in identifying and launching change. They are (1) admitting the behavior, (2) making a commitment to yourself to change the behavior, and (3) submitting yourself to God and the spiritual change that is about to take place. This means that one must embrace destructive behavior, manage the behavior, and replace it with processes that lead to empowerment, rational thinking, and a new fundamental for being successful in all we pursue.

When you change who you are, you will change the people and experiences you attract. The law of positive attraction only materializes with positive thoughts, plans, and actions. One must prepare for change by ensuring that our mentality is flexible enough to embrace it.

How do we achieve such a difficult task?

It's simple: We must tell the truth to ourselves and the ones around us. Honesty indeed is the best policy, but we must follow through on this policy by addressing exactly what we are honest about. We fall short because we stop short of what is needed to offer honest and healthy communication consistently with ourselves and others. You have a diagnosis, but – without honesty – you will not get the treatment needed to overcome what is ailing you. You are having a hard time curing you from yourself: self-doubt, self-pity, self-hate. **Someday starts now and, to change, you must envision being different – not different from anyone else, but different from whom you are now.** You need not go further in your vocabulary than the last profanity use nor any deeper in your mind than the last pain inflicted because you are about to be anew.

Change is about increasing your awareness about your identity. We all search for who we are until that light bulb, that "a-ha!" moment of clarity smacks us dead in the face with purpose. Change is about realizing and capturing those moments of clarity. However, all too often we ignore those moments out of fear, shame, or guilt. Very often, we think that we will conquer those challenges once and for all "someday." Yet, we fail to do so – and, as a result, "someday" never seems to arrive.

But someday is TODAY. Today is the day that you accept change. This day is special. Go mark it on your calendar so you can celebrate your anniversary next year. Change is about developing the vision you have for yourself by investing in the core that is you. Deepen your belief system by believing in yourself and the transformation that is about to happen. It all starts with the flick of a mentality switch … your mindset can make you stronger or it can kill you.

Are You Stronger Than Your Conditioning?

We have all been to the circus. I take my children every year. They have become accustomed to enjoying the lions, tigers, and bears. Every year it gets more entertaining and exciting. One year we got to go behind the scenes to see the different animals and meet the clowns. As we had finished interacting with the elephants, the trainer walked the elephants to another secluded area. As I observed my children interact with the clowns and everything else exciting, I couldn't help but notice what the elephant trainer was doing to secure the elephants. He drove some wooden stakes into the ground. The stakes were no bigger than 3 feet long and he drove each stake no more than 1 foot in the ground. He finished driving these stakes and began tying elephants to their own wooden stakes. I could not believe what I was witnessing because there was no way this pathetic stick could hold these enormous and powerful elephants. I excused myself from my girls and approached the elephants and their trainer. In a fearful yet chastising manner, I questioned the trainer on the safety of my children and all others who could be endangered by the sudden will and nature of these wild animals. In an attempt to calm my disbelief, anger, and confusion, the trainer said, "Sir, let me explain this to you: When this elephant was a baby, I tied it to a stick similar to this and then it could not move. As it grew older, I tied it to the same stake using the same method. As this creature of mass and power grew into adulthood, I continued to tie it to the same stake in the same manner. Over the course of time from a child to an adult, the elephant has grown in body but not in mind. I provided what was real in the beginning. The rope actually restrained her as a baby. As she grew, she created the illusion of restraint for herself. The elephant's will was defeated by what "appeared" to be. She defeated herself before even trying. She will never question her circumstance because in her mind it has been written that the rope is stronger than her will. Her frame of mind has been conditioned. The elephant does not know her own power or strength."

It is overwhelming that the conditioned mentality of one of the most powerful animals in the world would hold true today in the mentality of educated and vibrant women. Women are not giving themselves a chance. Women are defeating themselves mentally and by default are suffering physically. Simple, unhealthy affirmations of "I'm fat" or "I'm ugly" can reinforce the poor self-esteem that allows a person to give up. Please know that giving up takes as much energy as trying hard. It's all in your mind. Are you your own worst enemy? If you know this, it's time for a change. How long will you continue to be an enemy of yourself? How long will it take for you to learn to love you as you are? You probably will not believe it but, if you don't start loving yourself now, a nation is lost. You are the future.

Herbert Berry Williams

Mind Frame (CHANGE IT OR DIE)

Is your mind conditioned? What or who is your rope, trainer, and stake in the ground? Is it your mother, your boss, your significant other? Or is it simpler than that and you are your own worst enemy. Change is not easy.

There have been many in the past to try and fail.
There have been many in the past to try and succeed.
There have been many in the past to fail by not trying at all.
Which category will you fall into?

Change has been avoided purposely because it takes up too much effort. Change has also been avoided due to convenience, fear, lack of effort and lack of esteem. Is the processing of what is deliberately wrong for you easier than the processing of what is deliberately right for you? Is it easier to be weak and broken than it is to be God fearing and not man fearing and courageous?

It's a new day and it time for a change!

Here are a few more jewels to jumpstart change in your life.

Identify the opportunity /problem. Change starts with you. You have to identity some things. Who are you? What you will settle for? Who you will allow to be in your company? What is your worth and what do you want your worth to be?

Filter all information. You are a product of information you digest and you are a product of your environments you partake in. Change starts with filtering the truth of people, actions, and words.

Eliminate. This step is sometimes the hardest to do in change but elimination will result in being one of the most impactful steps in enhancing how you process decisions and relationships (people, action and words). Once you eliminate you can start fresh.

Build a support system of knowledge of self and surrounding and then a trusted support system of people, actions, and words.

Admit

One must realize that present, past, and future thinking patterns have the ability to bind us to a condition of limited realization, growth, and acceptance of the new you.

This conditioning will act as a barrier to the process of admittance. Do not be ashamed of the mistake … be proud of the decision to make a change. Do not let denial hold you hostage. The road to infinite possibilities does not begin until you say I have an issue … I want to address it … and I NEED SOME HELP.

9 Acknowledgements to FREE

1. I admit that I am powerless over my current situation — that my life and quality of life have deteriorated and are now unmanageable.
2. I choose to make a conscious decision to get to know God. I will create some type of spiritual balance in my life.
3. I will make a conscious decision to address mental and physical wellness.
4. I believe that God can renew my spirit to give me understanding of my worth and purpose.

5. I will take a collective inventory of mind, body, soul, and spirit and ask for healing and direction after I have been healed.

6. I will be consistent in taking daily inventory of self, starting with making rational and educated decisions based on fact.

7. I will educate myself and develop a relationship with myself that redefines standards and boundaries.

8. I will allow God to lead me to the treasures, rewards, and experiences that He says I deserve.

9. Having had a spiritual awakening as a result of these steps, I will carry this message to women in need of healing and renewal. I will also practice the principles of self-accountability, self-education, self-love, and love of God in all my affairs.

These nine acknowledgement statements will become foundational commandments on your road to recovery and healing. Please understand that recovery is not a bad thing or anything to be ashamed of. Recovery is weakness and irrationality leaving the body. To admit is power in and of itself. Admitting is the beginning of self-revolution. Admitting is the beginning of growth. Are you ready?

Love

I love to love And lately I've been feeling like love is in need of love So much hate I suffocate trying to breathe of love I keep my hand on the plow trying to sow seeds of love Hoping they blossom beautifully where the weeds once were because I feel that love is in need of love so much that for me to show love is imperative So poetically I profusely poured love into this narrative, informative, expose, persuasive Love related poetry by which I hope you are persuaded … to love Love intricately, intimately, intuitively all inclusively Extend your love to someone, love someone exclusively Love to be affectionate love to kiss, love to touch Find someone that doesn't love themselves enough and love that person too much To me love is like oxygen I simply could not breathe without it. I am so madly in love with love that I am happy to be mad about it Glad to be mad about it emphatically ecstatic about it And if you've ever experienced love you know that love has a magic about it If I could measure love in time I would become timeless with the passing of every minute And if I could swim in love I would go out so deep that it would be possible for me to drown in it Because true love is not shallow you have to get deep down in it And submerse yourself in love large enough for the universe to spin around in it I was told that love is blind so sometimes I love blindly Because if you love me at 10% its only right that I love you back at 90% Because some days you'll have to love me at 90 because I can only supply 10 But it's cool because you're my partner, my ace, my companion, my best friend but then Make no mistake: love does take work every day won't be easy there will be drama But I'm talking about that 50 year anniversary love like paw-paw loves grandmamma That kind of love endures and that kind of love matures and That kind of love is unconditional, reciprocal and reassures that love will save the day and love will be your crutch and if no one has told you today let me say I LOVE YOU Thiiiiiiiiiiiiiiiiiiiiiiiiiiiiiiiiiiiiiiiiiiiiiiiiiiiiiiiiiiiiiiiiiiiis MUCH

Se7en

Love Yourself!

Some women have never known what love is. Some women are afraid of love. Some women stop loving themselves when they start loving someone else. Some women do not know how to love. Love is a rich and complex dynamic that is often simplified and equated to the worth of material possessions and over emotionalized situations. We have reduced love to the standards of compromise, attention, sex, a rose, a ring. Love is intense. Love is grand but only if you treat it as such. Never bigger than life but sincere and real enough to develop a relationship, friendship, and interaction that is true, that was meant to be.

Love is a feeling and a void that cannot be filled with fly-by-night remedies. It will be hard, but the time for defining what healthy love is to you and knowing the limitations of what you will accept and will not accept in the form of love starts today. Why wait? Do not be influenced by the illusion of a timeout from loneliness. Define what love is, stay true to yourself and engage the quest or management of current love on your own terms. Look in the mirror, tell yourself you love you some you, and start loving yourself immediately. The love of self is one of the best loves you can receive.

Love Overboard

I stopped loving myself when someone else started loving me. Was it a mistake? Yes, a mistake I did not want to answer to. I found out that needing someone else to love me was worse than a drug addict's addiction to drugs. Needing to be loved can be an addiction …. love as a drug … who would have ever thought? In my addiction, I found myself drifting farther and farther away from self. My mind, body, and soul dissolved until I lost touch with myself, my reality. Instead of embracing the feeling of love and what could be, I overextended my emotions which resulted in the unhealthy need (addiction) of another. I became an option while he was my priority and I did not even mind. I put myself on hold … my friends on hold, goals on hold, dreams on hold, God on hold and no call waiting. It's ironic that it was me on the other end getting the busy signal (confusion), the voicemail (anxiety). I knew that this was not right but had no way out – or so it seemed, until one day no guidance and no direction spiraled into an out-of-control plea from the One I had been trying to ignore … GOD. This is what He told me as He rescued me from myself again: "When you do not have anyone to love you, learn to love yourself more. When you have someone to love and the love is not mutual, have boundaries." Boundaries are safety nets to the blindfolded hi-wire acts we walk while in love. PRIORITIES BACK INTACT, I PUSH ON. My mental armor will see me through my emotional weaknesses. Recharged and renewed in faith and head to the sky, I will do my best to balance the disappearing act of men, love, and self.

Some women exert all their energy into the wedding and are running on an empty fuel tank when it comes to the love and the marriage. Sometimes I have to ask myself which is more important to a woman – the wedding or the marriage? Marriage would last longer if women put as much business into the marriage as they did the wedding.

Being a Lover:

Is not just simple physical interaction. It encompasses all of the following elements:

1) Mental
2) Emotional
3) Exploration
4) Spontaneity
5) Communication
6) Knowing yourself
7) Stimulation outside of sex
8) Foreplay
9) Intimacy
10) Unselfishness

Learning Your Role as a Lover

Love is an emotion of strong affection and personal attachment. Love is also a virtue representing all of human kindness, compassion, and the unselfish loyal and benevolent concern for the good of another.

After experiencing various forms of love in negative and positive ways, I came to realize that to make something fluent and applicable in your life, you must have an understanding of its meaning, apply it in a positive and negative way, and have a grasp of reality based on your experiences. Then you must be able to decide what you must do to gain true, authentic love.

The first place someone experiences relationship is in the family: two or more people who share goals and values, have long-term commitments to one another, and usually reside in the same dwelling place.

If you have grown up in a broken or dysfunctional family as I did, you already have a distorted view of what love is from the start. Parenting is one of the most challenging jobs in the world and, when you have not received a good example of it, there can be a lot of trial and error when you become a parent.

I came from a single-parent household where I spent a lot of time with my siblings. My mother worked a lot. At our age, we should have been getting a sense of belonging, acceptance and identity. That is what I lacked and held an underlying need for, especially male validation.

My first relationship was 'young' love. I was eighteen and he was two years older than me. We both were products of low-income families. The substance of our relationship fed our need to belong and be accepted.

My next relationship was one of security. I dated a gentlemen 20 years my senior. I was about 25 years of age. This relationship was headed towards marriage, but I was not of a mature enough mindset to give him what he needed in a lover.

The position he held in my life delayed my maturity in the areas I needed to improve, such as being responsible financially. I also had not developed my own identity.

I was a people pleaser, meaning when in relationship I would do and be exactly what that person desired until I would realize how the shoe did not fit.

The unmet needs of our relationship [and his] complaining about my negative habits made me feel insecure about [not] being the woman who, at one time, met his desires [and this eventually] opened the door to my next relationship.

This relationship was a true rebound. You know his kind: You end up with him because the last guy you were with left you and wounded your heart so badly that he left you feeling so vulnerable that your behavior is now so reckless and you could really care less how your present actions will impact anyone else. As you can imagine, that relationship truly went nowhere fast.

In the next relationship, we intentionally were not trying to become serious. We were just 'kicking it' and leaving our options open. This guy lived a lifestyle of promiscuity and infidelity. He was so smooth that he knew how to affirm a woman in such a way where she would be willing to do just about anything whether she knew it was right or wrong.

After experiencing a lot of things in that relationship, it further contributed to my already low self-esteem. It truly deteriorated my self-worth.

Finally I decided to take a long-awaited break from relationships, filling my time with work, exercising and school. Have you heard of the saying, when you are not looking for someone they show up?

Well, that is what happened!

This relationship was something different. It was not about security or about me receiving ANYTHING from another person. I was free to be responsible for myself.

We were authentically experiencing each other's company with no expectations. After meeting and dating for a few months, it was revealed that we each had not long exited prior relationships and still needed time to heal.

I thought things were going well, but after dating this short period of time, he left without saying anything, stopped calling me and taking my calls.

By now, I was very attached emotionally, as well as physically, and desired an explanation for what was happening.

As a result of this, and the aforementioned relationships, I found [that] some of the most important tools in a relationship are being a good listener, knowing how to communicate and taking the time to truly observe who your mate is showing [himself] to be.

Another thing I think we ladies fail to realize is that the thing that gives us trouble with a spouse or mate in a relationship may be the very thing we need to look at in ourselves.

Despite the fact that our start was rocky, I did not hesitate when he wanted to rekindle things. We eventually ended up moving in together and decided to make a go of our union.

I was a single parent of a middle school aged son who until this point had only lived with me without his father or any other male figure in the same household.

My mate had no children of his own, though his last girlfriend had daughters; he had never had a 'son.'

Neither of us had thought about what this relationship would take or require in order for both of us to flourish.

I had been a single mother from a single-parent household. So everything I learned from my mother about relationships was to get with someone who can take care of you, and loves you more than you love them; and when the road gets rough or undesirable, if you choose to, you can always leave.

My mother married for security and was the dominating personality in the household, so I always found myself seeing male and female roles as being reversed.

My beau also grew up without his father and was put out of his mother's household at an early age. Therefore, neither of us knew our proper roles.

He was still finding his own identity as a man and learning what it took to be the head of a household. All this while I needed to be taught how to let go of wanting to lead and come under submission to his leading.

When challenges began to come at us as a family unit, we divided and faced them as the individuals we were.

My son began to disrupt our household for the lack of attention and the changes in our living status. Someone else was occupying time and space that was usually his. As my mate tried to advise me in this area, I would not listen because I felt, "What does he know? He has no kids."

The pressure of balancing a household of three compared to one was also something that was giving our relationship trouble. I only knew how to spend money, not budget it.

He rationalized my spending and made it comfortable for me not to tame these habits. Feeling unappreciated, he began to shut down emotionally because his needs were not being met in the dynamics of our household.

I guess he thought being alone again would be better, so he moved his things out and left without any warning. After this dramatic disruption to my household, the relationship was severely broken, and so was I.

He was gone for about two to three weeks and wanted to come back home. He was remorseful and was sorry. Unfortunately, the trust had been broken and things could never be the same. Things were no longer as they were when we started out.

We were in a rocky place from the beginning. We were two individuals who were not whole in our minds, bodies or souls. We were not stable in our own right, or making healthy lifestyle choices while having an understanding of what unconditional love meant.

Unconditional love overcomes arguments, separation, finances and anger. This type of love is only acquired through a flourishing growing relationship with the only one who has accomplished the act of loving unconditionally: God.

Tangela Russ

TRUE LOVE

We search for Love in some very unfamiliar places ... Confusing our own selves about Love, giving it many different Faces ... We invest in Love, we go all in for Love, some of us work, pray, and eat for Love ... Many of us Live for Love, are scared of

Love ... Not sure where we should find it sometimes, so we look in the Clubs for Love ... You got those that will die for Love, that same person will turn around and even Kill for Love, Steal for Love ... It's amazing to me how we get Hurt and Healed from Love ... We like Love in the Morning, and need Love to go to sleep at Night ... Sometimes couples Love, Love so much that all they can do is fight ... Some of us Love so hard we hurt ourselves ... Love to help others, but refuse to help themselves ... I know people that will even Pay for Love ... Disrespect themselves, just to stay with who they think they Love ... We will do all this for Love, look everywhere for it, except up above ... See, we are hard-headed and stubborn and want Love to be what we say it is ... We want that fairytale Love, the kind we learned as kids ... We Love our money, Love our cars, we Love reality TV, because we Love to live like the stars ... We will Love ourselves, Love our neighbor, but how many out there truly Love their Savior ... See, the same Love you have looked all over for, comes from the same God that has been there for you each time you have explored ... Each time that you failed, each time you gave up, each time you threw your hands up and said that's enough!!! God was there when you first found Love, when you got so deep in it, you drowned in Love... When you were a fool for Love, when you missed out on the One for you, because you were too cool for Love ... God was there when you divorced Love, when you cursed Him out for even giving you Love ... God stayed with you even when you said you would Love no more, and when your heart got broken again, it was God you called on as you fell to the floor ... All these times God has been around, and we always act like we never notice ... We fall in Love with everything in this world, except the One who loves us the closest ... So I say today on Valentine's Day ... Let us all agree to Love with no regard every day! And before putting all our faith into somebody else, let us all first learn to Love ourselves and then, maybe then, you can be loved ... But before you do that, you must first commit to the One up above, because when it comes down to it, God is love ... So until you and your loved one learn to love God, you will always wonder why your relationship feels odd ... God is the reason we can look at love as a beautiful experience, and not as a job... So let us remember every day to love God first, and ourselves next, and I guarantee He will work out the rest ... And when you are finally able to experience what True Love is, then you will see how much you have already been blessed! I Love You!

Joe P

Submit

- You need to be able to trust and depend on those you are submissive to specifically God, yourself, your mate, family, and friends. You are a creature of emotion but you have to will yourself to trust facts and information and not emotions.

Gut feelings are okay, but you still need the facts. Men and women lie – numbers and facts do not.

- Get comfortable with trusting God. God will allow you to trust yourself. Get more comfortable trusting God, and God will show you in whom you can put your trust and to whom you can submit. There is a saying: I asked God to protect me from my enemies and I started losing friends, mates, and pieces of myself. Be careful to whom you submit your time and trust. When you submit, you are investing trust. The wrong investment of trust can cause a lifetime of regret. Do not let your regret be another version of hindsight being 20/20. God will give you the maturity and wisdom to rule out the fake when you submit to his guidance. Once you have the power to do so, it is up to you. You will have the power to remove hindsight being 20/20 from your vocabulary and your life.

- Today we are changing the definition of submission. From now on begin submissive will resonate as a voluntary yielding to the will of clarity and rationality in God, self, health, family unit, and community.

Should I Submit?

Submission within a marriage means to render, obey, or exalt a self-humbleness to actively receive the guidance of another individual who is considered to be the leader of the household. We as women sometimes get confused with our role as wives. We were never designed to take on the role of a man, which is why we tend to get so emotional or have frequent meltdowns.

Men were designed to bear the armor for war, and we were designed to nurture, console, and be his helpmate. We replenish and build up the areas where the world has torn him down. My point is comparable to that of a king and queen. The King is the ruler, but it doesn't mean the queen's voice is irrelevant. Most kings resource and communicate with the queen. This sets true also for the president and the first lady of the United States. She must follow his lead and submit to his lead. This does not devalue her or make her less relevant.

Submission came hard for me the first time around within my marriage because, like most African-American women, my mother was the head of our household and submitting was nowhere in her vocabulary, actions or teachings to her daughters. My mother worked two jobs, managed the income, as well as had the final say on decisions. So, when I was of age to marry, submission was not in my plans. I was not about to surrender my autonomy to another person. It was more of a joke to me. Due to my ignorance on marriage, lack of exposure, and [young] age, the term "submission" was more of an alien, a sign of weakness and very irrelevant to me. I was taught to never let your right hand know what your left hand was doing. I did exactly that, kept my secrets to myself. My husband was not aware of my financial stance, decision making; nor was he in total control of rearing our children. Following his lead voluntarily was never my choice. I was following in the same footsteps as I was taught. I hindered my growth as a wife, mother, [and] leader, and my marriage suffered in that aspect of prosperity.

As time passed, I gained a better understanding of my duties as a wife per the religious aspect. I rebelled initially because I didn't feel like my husband was deserving of my full dedication as it related to giving him reign over my life as he saw fit. I didn't trust his judgment, nor did I agree with his rearing techniques.

Once I realized the things that are relevant in a marriage, it was too late for me to try to exercise it. By the time my marriage dissolved, I felt as if I was ready to make some changes within myself and gather a better understanding and significance of a marriage and the duties required of a wife and husband.

I remarried about a couple of years later, eager to be the best wife ever. We attended marital counseling. When the subject matter on submission was up for discussion, it was like being introduced to a new world because everything as I knew it was obsolete. I began to understand the husband is the leader and the wife is the help mate.

Ephesians 5:22-23 teaches: Wives, submit yourselves unto your own husbands, as unto the Lord. For the husband is the head of the wife, even as Christ is the head of the church; and he is the savior of the body.

So, I had to make a conscious effort to honor and obey my husband as I was designed to do. It is not the easiest thing to do. It definitely presents many challenges and sacrifice. It requires you to think and act selflessly. It has very little room for selfishness and presents quite a fight when you have to struggle with that. The flip side of this is your husband should be as attentive to his wife as he is to himself. Just because he is in the lead [role] and bears the responsibility of the family does not give him the right to neglect, ignore or mistreat his wife or family or downgrade her position as leader and equal partner in the business of marriage.

Ephesians 5:25 states: Husbands, love your wives, even as Christ also loved the church, and gave himself for it.

Once married, I humbly rendered everything to my husband and consulted with him prior to making major decisions. This was a huge impact on my [independence], but it eventually transformed my mindset to engage in interdependence. I was so accustomed to doing what I wanted to do when I wanted to do it without the seconded approval of another [human] being. For example, one day my sister asked to borrow a few hundred dollars. My usual response was "ok" and the money would be in her account. She wasn't expecting my response and I couldn't believe it was actually rolling off of my tongue either. My response was, "I would love to help you, but I need to speak with my husband in regards to what you are asking." Those dreaded words hit her hard. She was so upset with me. Her response to me was, "Since when do you need the approval of a n**** to give me money; it's never been a problem before. This n**** got you brainwashed. Where is your backbone and why does he have to know anyway? You have your own money!" As I held the phone to my ear, my heart dropped into my stomach. She made me feel as if my decision making was devalued and I relinquished my authority to my better half. I felt horrible. I mean I was hit below the belt so hard I almost cried. I tried to explain my case without sounding weak or worthless. At that very moment, I realized my dedication to my vows was being put to the test. This was lesson one. It required me to think beyond my emotions before acting irrationally to prove a point to someone I didn't vow a commitment to. I stood my ground. I didn't make that hasty decision prior to speaking with the head of my household. I felt really good within myself once I consulted with him. His response was along the lines of him trusting my judgment. We decided on a dollar amount that was feasible to loan to our relatives/friends without having to consult with each other.

This decision helped rebuild my self-confidence and value. It opened up a newfound appreciation for what we were desperately trying to build. We were reassured that effective communication actually works when it is demonstrated in an appropriate manner respecting both parties' points of view.

Let's talk about sex in the eyes of women. Most women can do without sex when the mental stimulation is not present. Mental stimulation, for the most part, is the basis for a great sex life. Sex is not supposed to be withheld from either husband or wife when they are in need to interact in that manner.

Most men on the other hand can have sex at any time without regards to how they may be feeling emotionally. It is our responsibility to fulfill his needs as it is his responsibility to fulfill our needs.

One day I had an urge to go through my husband's phone, due to the rise of my own insecurities. The old saying says when you go looking for trouble you will certainly find it. I quickly learned that my husband had been conversing with this particular female over the course of three years, which put them at a starting point prior to our union. My FBI techniques allowed me to find her home address, place of employment, name, and home number. Needless to say, this drama caused our relationship to turn sour. However, my feelings for this man did not change.

Mentally I was not in a place that allowed me to enjoy sex with him.

Initially, I was a non-participant during sex or any other intimate activities that would possibly lead to sex. I was mentally distraught. He was not disturbed by the situation and somehow continued to ask me for sex. I grew very angry with the fact that he was more fixated on sexing me than he was with consoling me or assisting me with the pain he had caused me. At that moment I knew something had to be done to make this better. At that time, the movie Fireproof was circulating. We watched the movie together and it got us to thinking about what really mattered to us and our marriage. I later learned that the "Love Dare" challenge book was a reality. I purchased the book and secretly worked on myself as I worked on saving our marriage. After all, I was still in love with my husband. I acknowledged the fact that we were human and made poor decisions when the flesh is leading at its best.

Marriage is an agreement among three. It is not hard. It is synonymous to a mother blessed with her child ... it must be nurtured because it is delicate ... it REQUIRES sacrifice, dedication and a willingness to learn ... it demands us to be taught how to LOVE unconditionally ... the trio consists of the Wisdom Influencer For Eternity (WIFE), the Head Unifier Sent By the Almighty (HUSBAND), and the one who Guides Our Destiny (GOD) ... Marriage is an agreement among three ...

On day 10 of the challenge we found the topic to be "Love is Unconditional." This was a very hard pill to swallow. It was now requiring me to look past his visible faults and acknowledge my invisible faults that he was unaware of. A passage read, "... love was based on feelings or circumstances rather than commitment. That's the result of building a marriage on Phileo love (the natural affection in all people for the appetite of the senses) or Eros love (sexual desire). There must be a stronger foundation than mere friendship or sexual attraction. Unconditional love, agape love, will not be swayed by time or circumstance ... you will experience an intimacy that cannot be achieved any other way." (Kendrick, 47-48)

At that moment I decided to reinstate my wifely duties and continue to have sex with my husband no matter what. I was forced to erase those negative thoughts from my head and replace them with positive, loving thoughts. When we performed our sexual activities, I mentally took myself to a place that would give us the optimal experience every single time. He was my husband and it was my responsibility to satisfy his every need as he is required to do for me. As crazy as it may sound, I vowed to submit unto my husband regardless of the situation we were battling with. I agreed to give him all of me without condition and that included sex. Eventually our sex life peaked and was better than before. It bought great enjoyment to him as well as myself because mental sex paired with physical sex was a combination unparalleled.

We often get caught up with pointing the finger or requesting change from the other person. Self-change and renewing of one's own mind is the hardest thing to do because it demands one's cooperation and dedication. The downfall is when change becomes too much for a person to bear and they began to feel unappreciated. This makes it easier for a person to revert back to their old ways. When I decided to take this venture, I didn't realize I was in for some much self-reflecting and improving. My self-enhancements caused him to re-evaluate his faults. I was able to witness change in him through my own self growth. It was truly a win, win. There is no need to request change from another if you are not willing to improve yourself as well. Love is found deep within and is selfless amongst others.

Dig deep to find the inner you. Dig deep to locate and confront your secret fears ...

Dig deep to capture the courage and armor needed to endure life's challenges ...

Dig deep to retrieve the jewels the enemy is desperately trying to steal ... Dig deep to gather the emotions that are yearning to be nurtured ...

Dig deep to meet honesty, trust and integrity for they are your friends ... Dig deep to greet relationship with open arms for it needs your attention for development and maturity ...

Now that you have dug in deep ... You have reached the core of your heart ... This is where your love lives ... It is now exposed and requires you to share ....

RED SUN

Commit

There are two necessary commitments you must develop concerning existence. They are the commitment to yourself and your commitment to God. Your commitment to your relationship with God should overwhelmingly exceed the commitment you made to your commitment to self because God will guide you to and through your destiny. When you are committed to God you can literally take your hands of the steering wheel when driving down the street of life. Let go and let God!

You should always commit to making you better so you can consistently make positive deposits into your existence on this earth. You also want to make you better so you can stand on your own with ease if and when that relationship ends. Your commitment will be the consistent investment and sacrifice into the foundation of your self-worth.

which will make you victorious. You will perish in the battle of life if you do not realize and internalize the importance of this investment. Commitment is not a phase. Commitment like *More Than A Rib* is a conscience lifestyle choice to be mentally and physically aware of your surroundings, the source of your motivations, and the definitive influencer in the choices your make.

You must learn to trust yourself. Commitment is balanced with trust. If you cannot trust, you cannot commit fully. If you cannot commit fully, we defeat the purpose of Admitting and Submitting. Be confident – not confident to the point of arrogance, but confident to the point that you have decided to trust yourself and trust God knowing that your hard work coupled with your faith in God will result each and every time in success.

Active commitment will move women from passive acceptance of life and its ups and downs to active non-acceptance of the process of settling, reducing standards, and status quo. Active commitment will place a value on self. Active commitment will reveal a reflection in the mirror. What do you see when you look in the mirror? I am doing something about it, I am making a difference in my own life, I am an example of you can do it too.

Commitment is scary because commitment manifests action. Action manifests results. Results manifest accountability and accountability brings us back to rational and irrational decision making processes. What are the drivers in your process: due diligence or a whim, facts or fiction, emotionally driven or numbers and data to support?

No matter the scenario, we must commit and the sooner the better. Once you commit to self, the battle is half over. The other half of the life's battles we are confronted with are things we have no control over anyway. The good news is that investment in self through mental and physical wellness, the constant mental uploading (self-education) and downloading (educating others) of information and the value you place on yourself will balance these battles out. Some you will win and ad some you will lose. That is life. You have to know yourself to place a value on yourself. You have to invest in yourself by committing to yourself to increase your worth. Commitment is key. We have looked at the foundation of growth through admitting, submitting, committing and affirmations. Our next step is examining 9 pillars that represent the next steps of your journey towards enhancement, enrichment, and evolution of self.

What Needs to be Understood

More Than a Rib is here to be a resource for women to evolve and improve from the current status quo. This information resource will soon allow millions of strangers to interact, embrace, and support one another through encouragement, dissemination of information (education), and sisterhood.

We try and try to make rational decisions daily. Our ability to make rational decisions on a consistent basis are usually directly or indirectly tied to one of the nine circumstances or conditions: sexual violence, divorce, domestic violence, single-parent households, drug abuse, finance, lack of faith (which is constantly tested after going through these trying events), difficulty in knowing how to grow and transition, and poor choice in people, places, or things.

Through focus groups and surveys, we have concluded that all the above circumstances influence rationality and irrationality. We have no control over some events in life. These events are usually when someone has taken advantage of our age, physical, and/or mental limitations. We are unable to defend ourselves because the decision was not ours to begin with. Some decisions are forced because of the perception of the situation(oasis) or time restraints associated with making a decision. You can have control, but ultimately be pressured into a decision because of circumstances. Irrational decisions come from making decisions under duress (e.g., anger, revenge, love, entrapment) and not thinking the consequences of these decisions through carefully.

It is time to understand your hurt and pain. It is time to turn your hurt and pain into strength and triumph. You can never forget that expressing your testimony can be therapeutic for you. You must also realize that there is power and healing in your testimony for someone else. It is time to be educated. Be loosed from ignorance and realize that help, preventative measures, and proactive practices are available to ensure healthy and productive decision making, relationships, and mentalities.

Studies have shown that irrational decisions by women have been driven by anger, happiness, spontaneity, regret, fear, revenge ... EMOTIONS. Studies have also shown that many of these emotions stem from a dysfunction that is subsequently inherited due to an inability to process the situations encountered, processing of feelings and emotions, and a lack of a strong support systems and resources needed to overcome and manage trauma.

These acts are having an impact on present and future thinking patterns in women (and men). Betrayal and trust issues are roadblocks that are the result of rape, domestic violence, single-parent households, divorce, and drugs (the latter will be addressed in the next installment). We will explore these topics to educate and provide information and resources that can be useful in understanding, preventing, and overcoming the fears associated with these topics.

Rape is the act or crime committed by one person forcing another person to take part in sexual intercourse through threat or use of violence. Rape: Ravishment, Violation, an Outrageous Force.

Domestic violence, also known as domestic abuse, spousal abuse, battering, family violence, or intimate partner violence, is defined as a pattern of abusive behaviors by one partner against another in an intimate relationship.

Domestic violence defined has many forms including physical aggression or assault, threats of sexual abuse, emotional abuse, controlling or demeaning, intimidation, stalking, passive covert abuse and economic deprivation.

Relationship defined is the way in which two or more things are connected, or the state of being connected. In 1891, James wrote that a person's self-concept is defined by the relationships we endure with others. God created us with relationship in mind. Father, mother, lover and friend, sister, daughter, son and brother: each one of us has the desire to feel certain, deep down in our hearts, that someone loves us, cares for us, and has our best interest at heart.

Babies, Girls, Females, Ladies and Women are distinctively and wonderfully made as Precious, Fragile, Virtuous and Special beings. Men are opposite in nature and are wired differently. Men are made in God's image as protectors, providers, promoters, priests and givers. His creativity in women made them more of His heart, love, emotions, nurturing, birthing, and receivers of His entire valor. It is a shame that worldly behavior continues to separate man from woman, father from children, and society from church. Is clarity in the Windex© or is it clear as mud that the dysfunction of family is where the improper and immature behavior of at least one parent can have damaging effects on the growth of individuality and healthy relational skills among individual, family, and society as a whole?

Rape

Sexual assault is an act of violence that is by definition against the victim's will. The victim is forced to submit to genital, oral and/or anal sexual acts and often to other aggression, abuse and degradation. The attacker controls the situation by the use of physical force, threats of harm and intimidation.

As a result, women often experience severe psychological effects. The way the victim copes with the trauma of rape is dependent on several factors. These include her ego, inner strength, social network support, life cycle stage and the way she is treated as a victim. The most common and lasting effects of rape involve mental health concerns and diminished social confidence. These concerns can affect rational decision making and personal interaction.

Looking for Love in all the Wrong Places

There is no way to sugarcoat it. I was raped when I was 13. A female friend of my mother twisted my mind so badly that I thought I could fly without wings.

There was nothing you could tell me that I did not already know. I knew the answer to everything and, until that day, I could not be defeated. On that day, the inebriation of sweet nothings and alcohol stole my youth and by default made me the woman that I thought I was and that I am today.

It is funny because back then I thought I found what I had been missing in my single-parent household. I was missing the father figure that should have been loving, guiding, and inspiring me and saying, "You are beautiful ... you can do anything." Instead, I got the work-a-holic mother that let my friends, after school specials and my attitude that she could not deal with raise me.

My rape was my first female experience that turned me inside out and upside down. I saw her sparingly after what happened, though she never tried anything again.

It was strange because when she did not try anything, I felt like I did something wrong. Maybe I was ugly. Maybe I was not good enough. Twisted right?

The mind of an adolescent craving ... wanting ... needing ... love. I had never been with a boy before, but I fantasized about them all the time.

Other than my rape, I had never been with a girl but now I fantasized about them, too. I did not know if was coming or going for a few years. The rape had me exposed to the harsh reality of lesbianism.

Confused, lonely and clueless, I wandered throughout my teenage years barely passing my grades, slowly dying from the hurt of not having a father and a mother.

A mother is someone who cares just because, and my mother acted like parenting was a job that she clocked in and out for. The resentment I felt drove me to drink and look for other ways to suppress my pain, anger, and emptiness.

To me, alcohol and unprotected sex go hand in hand when you are a young teenager that will do anything to be loved and accepted. I look back now and wonder how I survived and know that is only by the grace of God that I can recollect some of the nightmares I am about to share in two pages or less.

I dated both guys and girls. There was no specific preference. If the right thing was said or whoever had the right money, had the right weed, drove the right car ... I was pretty much theirs, at least for the day, a weekend, a week, a month or however long it took for me to realize that the situation was not numbing my pain anymore.

I dropped out of school; but, later on with direction and help from a guidance counselor I knew, I got my GED. Life was not good but I was not dead. That is the way I had to look at it.

I moved out of my mother's house and lived from pillar to post, a couch one day, and the back seat of a car the next. Unstable, unwilling, and undetermined, I lived my life selfishly for the next few years until I bumped into a moment of truth. (This is when you come to that fork in the road that says up, down, left, right, heaven or hell … what do you choose?)

It is messed up that my moment of truth was caused by a rude awakening that changed my life forever. One night while out drinking with a male friend, we got invited to [the house of] one of his friends.

I reluctantly went, but knowing that there was going to be alcohol, pills, and weed there made the situation much more tempting.

When we got there, there were some more guys and more girls and the party was going on! I was very drunk at this point – so much so that I passed out and woke up the next morning in a bedroom with no clothes on.

Do I remember what happened? No. How did I get here? Where's the friend that I came with? Did I have sex? Was it consensual? Was I raped again?

I did not know the answers to any of those questions. I tried to gather my thoughts, get my things, get dressed and let myself out. I tried to put the pieces together but could not figure it out.

Month one, I am still at a loss for thoughts. Month two, I find myself at a loss for words. Month three, I have lost my will and am depressed.

As I try to put the pieces together, I contemplate suicide but I cannot keep the thought in my mind for throwing up every other hour ... [I thought:] Why does this keep happening to me? Is this what life is supposed to be about?

I did not have any health insurance but I had to go see why I kept vomiting. I told the physician [that I had] been feeling funny for the past few weeks, throwing up, and [with] an upset stomach.

The doctor informed me that he must run some tests, but from the sound of things I may be pregnant. Pregnant?

I had been doing drugs but I had not had sex with anyone for at least 2 or 3 months .... While I sat wracking my brain, the incident at the party came to my mind!!

The doctor come back and said that he had some good news and some bad news and then asked which would I like to hear first? Of course I replied the good news and that is when he told me I was pregnant for sure. I was overwhelmed with a mix of emotions. I did not know who the father was; I was very confused and dazed ...

It must have shown on my countenance because he asked was I okay because now he had to give me the bad news.

In my mind, [I thought: What] bad news, what could it be? He then told me that they had found a strand of HIV and it was a great possibility that my baby might contract the virus as well.

My heart sunk. Reality sent a scream through my soul that still frightens me to this day. My moment of truth was here and it was now or never that I had to decide what was right and what was wrong.

I knew what was wrong, but I kept choosing the wrong path anyway. Do I keep the baby or get an abortion? I had never soul searched or prayed before but that is what I started doing right there in the doctor's office. With tears rolling down my eyes, I decided to keep the baby.

I decided it was time to get my stuff together. It was time to stop being that little, raped 13-year-old girl and start being a woman. Funny ... HIV, no job, no place to live, no education, no direction, and no example of what a mother should be ... Lord knows my lesbian mother did not leave or give any advice .....

I decided right then and there that I was going to make a change. Either I was lying to myself or I was going to be a blessing to someone. I can now sit here today at 35 and tell you that I am a blessing. I never knew that all you had to do was ask. That day in the doctor's office I asked God to take me and do what His will was.

In the blink of an eye, I found the doctor giving me necessary information to survive. I had to work at getting into programs. I did not even have an ID at 22 ... looking back all I can say is wow!!

I had to convince myself that my baby was worth it. More importantly, I had to convince myself that I was worth this. I had to ask myself could I love if I had never been loved or could I be an example if my whole life had been jacked up because of my poor choices and decisions.

No father because I did not know who the father was. Can I be what my mother could not be? Both a mother and a father?

I have HIV; will I ever find someone THAT I CAN LOVE AND THAT WILL LOVE ME BACK UNCONDITIONALLY?

There were so many questions and not enough answers or so the devil would make it seem. Throughout life I learned that education, patience, and planning come at a price called discipline and honesty ... mainly being honest with yourself!

I was never willing to take on the responsibility of being honest with myself and loving myself. I was always looking for the love of another first. How insane is that?

In this moment of truth, I decided that I would have to dig deep and love me and this child I was about to bring into the world. Through the leads from the hospital, I was able to get information and help that I never knew was afforded to me.

One door after another opened for me. I am still amazed at knowing all I had to do was ask. I asked God and He showed up and showed out.

Program after program and blessing after blessing is all I can say. By His grace, 13 years later I can say that my twins (boy and a girl) are healthy and were not infected with the HIV virus.

I was enrolled in a program that deals with experimental drugs to fight the HIV virus. I am currently on that medication and it's working well.

My living arrangements are stable. We do not have much, but we have what I lacked while growing up and that is love. I am the mother and the father.

I kiss it when it hurts. I discipline them when needed. I love and educate them unconditionally because I know that the lack of love can lead to "LOOKING FOR LOVE IN THE WRONG PLACES."

The world is crazy ... Your children will always have an opinion on how they should be raised. We need to stay in the parent lane and parent.

They may be get angry, but constantly check on your children (by any means necessary) .... you never know who or what they are doing. My life is not where I want it to be, but it is definitely going in the right direction.

I used to let life pass me by, but now I live life and I live it out loud. There is no silver lining in this story, but there is a blessed and changed life as a result of it.

Sometimes it takes something to shake the foundation and create change, and for me it was HIV and my unplanned pregnancy.

Do not be like me. If you need help, ask for it. There are many public programs to assist you in getting information that can set you up for success.

National AIDS Hotline: English service (7 days a week, 24 hours a day) 1-800-342-AIDS (2437) Spanish service (7 days a week, 8 a.m. till 2 a.m. eastern time) 1-800-344-7432 TDD service for the deaf (10 a.m. till 10 p.m. eastern time, Monday through Friday) 1-800-243-7889

RAINN (Rape Abuse Incest National Network): 1-800-656-(4673)HOPE

Suicide Hotline: 1-800-273-8255 (TALK)

City info line 211 or 311 (most cities)

Brittany Renee

I shook hands of not only a stranger,

But the hands of a 15 year old murderer.

A killer, along with being a rape victim

I feel for her.

For one, she can't even tell her story.

She lives life in a hurry.

She just trying to pass time.

Because she doesn't fully understand her sentence.

15 doing 25 is a long time.

You do the math.

By the time she's released, she'll be 40.

Which she has to utilize the rest of that time making up to her daughter who's always felt

Avoided,

It's sad.

25 years is time that she can never get back.

And the judge, he ain't even cut baby girl no slack.

She lost the rest of her life just trying to get revenge back.

But is it really her fault?

Doing something she was taught.

The 1st law of survival is Self Defense,

But she got charged with Assault.

With a deadly weapon.

And he lived 2 days after,

But as soon as his lungs decided to collapse on him,

It was the end of both of their chapters.

Murder was the case that they gave her.

Now she goes from recess, to recreation

From public schools to no visitation

Like really ...

Now although what she did was tragic,

Just look at the situation and exactly how it happened

This was her own Daddy.

A registered sex offender

She wasn't even supposed to be living with him

But now she has to suffer with the consequences

Playing tit for tat got her living with her hands behind her back

And as far as her mother,

Who doesn't really know now how to love her.

Gave up the baby to the state because her daughter murdered her husband.

It's crazy.

I just wanted to hug that baby.

She was only 15.

She don't even know what all that time mean.

She looked me straight in my eyes and asked me,

Do you know how hard it is for me to sleep at night?

Can you imagine how hard it is for me to dream?

Knowing that the first time I had sex was with my Daddy who forced me

Then I had a baby I never even seen.

Can you imagine being me?

There was nothing I could say to make this baby feel that everything would be ok.

I was lost for words.

Attempting to picture myself as her

But I couldn't do that too long, because that shit hurts.

As if she was only living to be cursed.

Living a life full of punishment over something she didn't even deserve.

And still the judge had no remorse.

That's just the way the cookie crumbles.

Now she's no longer Brittany Renee,

She's now just another Number.

Statistic

But let's just be realistic,

What would you do if your parents were touching you every night

And how would you deal with it.

But there is no gray area

Only White and Black

She lost her childhood,

Her virginity, her Dad,

And 9 times out of 10 when she gets out,

She won't be able to get her Kidd back.

Her name is Brittany Renee

And this story is true.

Never judge a person on their situation

Because you never know when the offs are going to be against you

Nikki Da Kidd (LaShonda Williams)

Domestic Violence

Domestic violence, also known as domestic abuse, spousal abuse, battering, family violence, and intimate partner violence (IPV), is defined as a pattern of abusive behaviors by one partner against another in an intimate relationship such as marriage, dating, family, or cohabitation. Domestic violence, so defined, has many forms, including physical aggression or assault (hitting, kicking, biting, shoving, restraining, slapping, throwing objects), or threats thereof; sexual abuse; emotional abuse; controlling or domineering; intimidation; stalking; passive/covert abuse (e.g., neglect); and economic deprivation. Alcohol consumption and mental illness can be co-morbid with abuse, and present additional challenges in eliminating domestic violence. Awareness, perception, definition and documentation of domestic violence differ widely from country to country, and from era to era. Domestic violence and abuse are not limited to obvious physical violence. Domestic violence can also mean endangerment, criminal coercion, kidnapping, unlawful imprisonment, trespassing, harassment, and stalking.

She was having an emotional cardiac arrest and there was no one there to perform mouth to mouth, no defibrillator in sight. Her time clock had been ticking ... 15 years of her mother's example, 7 years of her sister's example, and 2 years 3 days 5 hours and 18 seconds of looking at her own reflection had mentally and physically drained her. She had seen her mother and her sister go through the same abuse in relationships. She knew better or at least that is what she wanted friends and family to think. "I can change him, just you wait and see," she secretly pined in her mind. The pride and satisfaction of proving the naysayers wrong about the potential for her marriage to fail was all that mattered. At one point, her desire to sustain the marriage was fueled by tears, prayers and I'm sorry.

Never a new page in her book, but instead a quick and fast road to a slow recovery of ego, lips, and eye. Sunglasses and excuses always prepared for neighbor, the coworker, herself. She had to believe it to live it. Convincing herself that he loved her was easier than convincing herself that she could continue to love him and make excuses for his behavior. It seemed that she talked herself into loving someone who did not know the meaning of love and hate and, more so, how to express those feelings in a healthy manner. The representative he sent to hook, line, and sink her into his dysfunction did an exceptional job; standing ovations were in order for the performance of what he knew as life. His insecurities were the brick to the mental and physical prison she lived in. He had been abused himself as a child. The break-up, pain and R.I.P to come out of this was inevitable from the first ill display of fists over conversation.

She was packing her last bag as his key turned the lock. Her plans to escape the prison of her home were foiled by the uncertainty of spontaneity. Tonight he wanted to surprise her and make up for the fingers around her throat from Thursday, the bitches and whores that she was on Wednesday, the coming home at 5 am in the morning on Tuesday, and the opened hand slap because her promotion outweighed his third disciplinary write-up on Monday. He had so much to make up for, but she could not take the empty gestures anymore.

She had a plan if something like this would happen, but the fear and passion in the air erased the plan from her abused being. Mind, body and soul were fed up and aligned and ready for what would happen next. The door flew open and she was still frozen in the same position that she was in when she first heard the door begin to unlock. Fear and anxiety took over as she knew he would try to stop her from leaving one way or another. "Honey, I'm home - where are you?" He walked through the bedroom door to see suitcases packed and her frail and petrified body on the side of the bed. He said, "What are you doing?" as he continued to approach her. She knew what was in store. She remembered saying stop, don't come any closer as anger in his voice and the barely suppressed aggression erupted from his unaddressed pain. His hurt threatened to overtake him at any minute. She knew that he could not control himself; she knew what she had to do. She did not remember the 6 shots fired, the blood on her clothes, and the smoke coming from the barrel until the police were taking her away in cuffs as the neighbors looked on. It was too late. Her actions to stay were stronger than her will and thoughts of leaving. As she faced 25 to life, she realized that her desire to stay was an illusion held together with a needle with no thread.

It's never too late to leave and there are free resources out there for you. She should have left and you can leave too. We put energy into situations that are over before they start. She knew this but was driven by proving someone wrong. She knew because of what he had shown her time and time again leading to their marriage. When someone shows you who they are, take it at face value and act accordingly. God is in the people changing business. You cannot change people; people have to change and want better for themselves. She did not have a child to be affected by this situation, but children are usually always in the middle and affected the most. Always keep your and your child's safety guarded in relationships that have the potential for verbal and physical abuse. The way you handle this may affect how your child handles his or her situation if confronted with one.

Domestic violence is growing and is growing rapidly among our youth. Youth are bringing home too many school lessons of improper methods of handling emotions into their daily dynamic. The future does not look good. We have to change the direction of young men and women. We must provide alternative methods of coping and being successful in and outside of negative environments. We must reach her early and instill her worth early so she knows that she is here by design. She has been and will always be special. She has a torch to carry and a legacy to continue. Sometimes, she needs help to continue.

If you need help, remember computer use can be monitored and is impossible to completely clear. If you are afraid your internet and/or computer usage might be monitored, please use a safer computer and/or call the National Domestic Violence Hotline at 1–800–799–SAFE (7233) or TTY 1–800–787–3224.

If These Walls Could Talk

if these walls could talk they would say
"I don't know if it was her
& I don't know if it was him
all I heard was
I'm into noun changes
and nouns are-
persons, places, and things
So I'm changing the things I do
The places I go
& the person I do
starting with you
I got a beautiful train of thought
Instead of us growing old together
how about we grow old apart
I should have never given you a second
chance to make a first impression
cuz going back to your ex is like...
taking a bath
but putting the same clothes on

and you must not understand

I'm like 9 different types of crazies

and next time you put your hands on me

you're liable to meet one of them

they gonna find your body in the attic

the attic gonna be in the basement

the basement gonna be in the attic

the violence echoing off the cabinets

the cabinets shaking the paintings

the paintings are changing faces

can you see the wedding pictures mugging you yet

now what used to be a Kodak moment

is now posing a threat

If these walls could talk

They would say

"I don't know if it was her

& I don't know if it was him

but all I heard was

Close the hole in your face

stop talking to me

It's a difference between listening and just waiting to

speak Ima tell you what God loves and that's the truth

you can't play crazy with somebody that ain't playing

you living in a paradox

why?

cuz you drinking poison but expect me to die

you failed to realize we belong together

hurt people hurt people

fill in the blanks

student

and I'm here to teach you how to love somebody to death

so stop acting like I'm giving you hell

when all I gave you was Legos

hell, you built it yourself

just wait 'til you get old and senile

maybe then you'll see now

every blow that you receive is a favor

If it wasn't for the pain you wouldn't know you was alive

so ego to blame it on the evil

but sometimes it's not the enemy

it's the Inner me

if these walls could talk

they would say

I can hear them sirens

so let me file my statement

I heard some punches being thrown

Scratches around a neck

brown eye turned black

then the reflection in the mirror

turns its back

Somebody's ears are ringing

a lip is split

if Badu can view it from a window seat

it looks like an Ike and Tina skit

what a haunting sequel

if I had sight

you'll swear you seen dead people

knots to the back of the head

when pots and pans fly

who would have thought for the low price of $19.99

they would be used for more than just deep frying

he in the back of the ambulance

and she in the back of the police car

so Let's hear it for New York

them red and blue lights

Will inspire you

to do what?

the women are in doubt, but statistics are the proof

that 50 % of domestic violence really comes from you

Khalid

Divorce

Divorce (or the dissolution of marriage) is the final termination of a marital union. Divorce can be caused by many things and the consequences of divorce can affect all stakeholders involved (wife, husband, and children). Mental conditions of depression, anxiety, anger, guilt, and resentment can have life-changing effects on decision making and interaction with others. Studies show that divorce can have an impacting influence on relationships, academic achievement and job performance. Divorce needs to be managed with care concerning the mental strength and capacity of those involved. Do not be afraid to seek mental health assistance if you or your child experience(s) challenges from a current or past divorce. It is never too late to seek help, and there are plenty of free resources in your community.

DIVORCE …. Why It Should Be Your Last Alternative

It's one thing to say "let's not divorce." It's quite another to decide what you're going to do to save your marriage. There are several alternatives to divorce. The choice you and your spouse make will depend on your tolerance for change, your desire to be together or apart, and what you can afford.

The first alternative is to do nothing. No, really. You can choose to remain in your marriage even though it is an unhappy one - that is, if you decide you can live with the disappointment of an unsatisfying marriage more easily than you can live with the pain, expense, and disruption of divorce.

This may seem to be a strange choice, but you should know that many, many couples have made the decision to opt for a so-called "parallel marriage," probably many couples whom you know. Although they may not have "happy" marriages in the traditional sense, they have evolved a relationship that allows both of them to live pleasant, reasonably fulfilling lives.

The first step is an emotional one. It is the step we all have to take when coming to the decision to divorce. The first thing you should ask yourself is, do you really want a divorce? Next, you should make sure that you have done all you can to try to solve the problems in your marriage and salvage the relationship with your spouse.

I strongly believe that if you have children to whom you are morally obligated, you should do all you can to save your marriage. Divorce is not a decision to make lightly. It is not a decision that you make when feeling overly stressed and it is not a decision to make if you are dealing with depression.

My heartfelt advice to anyone thinking about this is to seek couples counseling, talk to your clergy, talk to your spouse about the problems as you see them, and be willing to work at saving your marriage before walking away from the marriage.

Today, we live in a throwaway society. We have become people who quit when the going gets tough. Unless you are suffering abuse or serial infidelity, the commitment you made to your spouse and marriage should be the most important thing in your life. It should be the thing you work hardest to maintain.

How do you know when your marriage has reached the point of no return? I asked myself some key questions before making the decision to file for divorce.

Was there even a marriage to begin with? If your marriage has never been anything more than two people living together and getting their own needs met, then divorce may be the answer. Marriage is a unified coupling of two people who work for the best interest of the relationship. Married couples work together for the good of the relationship. If there is no "couple," only two people fighting for their own needs, then now would be a good time to either commit to changing the dynamics of the relationship or part ways.

What is motivating you to divorce? Are you hoping that a divorce will mean your spouse will start treating you better? Maybe they will realize what they have lost and make the changes you need them to make? If so, you are divorcing for the wrong reasons. Divorce will only promote conflict, not resolve it.

Is it divorce you want, or are you just threatening divorce? Are you angry at your spouse and threatening divorce out of frustration over the problems in the marriage? Do you use threats of divorce to get your way or as a means of having power over your spouse? Are you frustrated and feel that threatening divorce will finally get your spouse's attention and they will take you seriously? If it is solutions you are looking for, threatening divorce will not get you where you want to be. Again, you need couples therapy for that. If your intent is divorce, however, then stop threatening and take a mature, informed step in the right direction. Do you still have feelings for your spouse? Have your feelings diminished, or are you feeling powerless over a problem in the marriage and, due to this, there is a lack of emotional closeness? If there are still feelings of love and affection, then you should work on the relationship before deciding on divorce.

Is your decision to divorce based on emotional reaction or true self-awareness? If you are ready for divorce, you will have let go of any emotional attachments you have to your spouse. These include good and negative feelings that often come into play during marital conflict. Deciding on divorce at a time when you are overwhelmed with emotions won't solve problems. It generates problems and compounds any hurt and frustration you may be feeling.

Unless you can look at your spouse as an individual who deserves your respect, even during the divorce process you are asking for trouble. If you cannot, the process will be riddled with frustration, anger and distrust of your spouse's motives. All a divorce will ultimately do is end your marriage and split apart your family.

If you want a change in the dynamics between you and your spouse, divorce is not what you want.

Something to think about: Once you have divorced, your spouse is free to form emotional attachments to others. If that thought is uncomfortable, think twice before making a decision.

What Led to My Divorce

My spouse and I decided that the way divorce would need to work to meet our needs, including the need to have private health insurance, was that living in the same home with one another would be easier than living with all the consequences of divorce.

We drew up specific but informal "marriage continuation" plans, including detailed arrangements for my ability to separate myself completely from him when he was drinking, violent, cheating and cursing me out.

It's certainly not the best solution for all troubled marriages. I was a firm believer in counseling. My marriage was in serious trouble and it was truly our only hope of saving it.

Counseling had the potential to help, but the problem would be our ability to change the way the two of us related to one another. The thought of it hurt almost as badly as divorce. We were not prepared for that.

A trial separation allowed me to sense if I truly wanted a divorce. I could experience some of the feelings of separation without making a final commitment to divorce.

I saw that the main advantage of our trial separation, of course, as being it was easily reversible. Beyond that, it took just as much negotiation as an actual divorce and maybe every bit as painful.

In fact, it made my pain worse because it prolonged the uncertainty of divorce. Nevertheless, we wanted to use a trial separation to give ourselves time to reflect on things. Could we truly live with the actual decision to divorce?

We made certain arrangements regarding our bank accounts and credit cards, what freedoms we would allow each other to form or carry on, such as new relationships, and how often we would re-evaluate our separation.

From my own personal experience, when a woman serves a man with divorce papers, she already has plans for her future and there is virtually nothing you can do to win her back.

I am not implying that all women who instigate divorce are having affairs, but women typically don't file for divorce unless they have something or someone else already lined up.

If you have been served divorce papers, try to find out why he wants out of the marriage. Don't argue, don't get mad, and don't accuse him of wrongdoing. Ask him to tell you why he wants out. Don't interrupt him, and listen closely to his reasons. I don't want to give you false hope, but there still may be time to save your marriage. If there is a chance for reconciliation, you BOTH must be willing to work at it; it can't just be one-sided.

The Consequences of Staying

Many people who stay in a bad marriage know that their marriage was over long before they left.

Misguided Reason #1 to Stay in a Bad Marriage: The Kids

If you are in a high-conflict marriage, staying in it "for the kids" has long-term effects. This decision will do more harm than good. You need to be able to face your children's pain and be there to help them cope.

If you are the one wanting the divorce, you will also have to deal with the pain of others. Do not allow their pain to make you feel guilt for pursuing a divorce.

Of course, children should be born into a loving two-parent home, preferably as a result of a marital relationship; or, if children were born out of wedlock, they would be adopted and raised by generous, caring couples.

Society assumes that children need this type of stability in order to thrive. However, society has changed, and so have attitudes towards marriage and children. Society no longer assumes that married parents are the norm.

At the same time, I affirm the wisdom and value of traditional practices. Children do better when raised in a home where their parents are married.

The three most significant reasons children are raised without the benefit of married parents are unwed pregnancy, cohabitation, and divorce.

Children of divorce experience lasting tension, as a result of the increasing differences in their parents' values and ideas. Divorce can mean a loss of dreams and goals. Even if you are positive a divorce is what you want, you need to have a support system in place to help you and your children deal with the stresses associated with divorce.

For the unhappily married couples, it seems to be more about the quality of the relationship than having the relationship itself. Women in unhappy relationships and women who divorce but are still emotionally tied to their ex-husbands have much weaker immune systems than the women who are in happier relationships or happily out of them.

In the 24 hours after a huge fight, both men and women show a significant decline in immune system functioning. Marital stress is linked to heart disease in women who suffer from chest pains; they are reported to have the highest levels of marital stress and are nearly three times as likely to suffer a heart attack or require a bypass.

There is no similar correlation between heart disease and marital stress for men. If you want a change in the dynamics between you and your spouse, it is not divorce that you want.

Parents' marital unhappiness and discord negatively affect their children's well-being, but so does the experience of going through a divorce. Getting a divorce is one of the most traumatic experiences a person can face. The end of a relationship feels like a death for some, but for others it feels like a new beginning.

Depending upon the circumstance, it can feel as if a heavy weight has been lifted, or it can feel like all is lost. It is important to focus on the positive aspects of getting a divorce instead of maintaining a negative outlook and sinking into deep depression. In fact, it can be the beginning of a whole new life.

Getting a divorce is not the end of the world and can have benefits when solutions have been tried. Your attitude will determine what kind of life you will have after the divorce.

Will you be strong, take responsibility and let go of any anger and resentment? Or, will you remain bitter, resentful and feel like a victim? The attitude you choose to live with will determine not only the kind of divorce you will have, but also the quality of life you have after you divorce. Are you able to act in a mature way? Although I do not think divorce is always the answer, when it becomes the only option, the following benefits of getting a divorce can lift the spirits and provide an entirely new perspective on a sad situation.

We all make mistakes and taking chances is a requirement of life. One of the benefits of getting a divorce is newfound freedom. A great weight is lifted and life will eventually present many new and exciting opportunities. It might feel like the end of the world at first, but everything will work out for the best when the marriage is definitely over.

The benefit of life without hatred, if it was a part of the marriage, is one of the best benefits of getting a divorce. Life is too short to live with continual hatred and turmoil. When the marriage is over, more than likely the selfish former spouse will move on to another unsuspecting individual until that person has had enough. They will never find contentment or anyone that will put up with their bad behavior for as long as you did.

Another one of the great benefits of getting a divorce is the opportunity to find new and lasting love. No one should jump right back into a relationship after a divorce. This might equate to jumping from the frying pan right into the fire. Until the pain of the divorce is over, you should think long and hard before considering another relationship.

Otherwise, good judgment may be tainted by the desire to be wanted and loved.

If someone had told me I would have been married and divorced six times, YES, that's what I said – 1, 2, 3, 4, 5 and 6 –, I would not have walked away from my past husbands, I would have run like hell!! Life is not always fair, and someone that once seemed like a Prince or Princess Charming in the beginning could turn out to be a loser in every sense of the word.

Exploring the benefits of divorce when no hope for reconciliation exists is certainly better than focusing on everything that went wrong. It is best not to waste time trying to figure other people out – unless of course you are a psychiatrist.

I said I would never marry again. I actually might not, but if the right person comes along, why should I spend the rest of my life alone just because I was married six times and encountered a cheater in every aspect of life?

The sun will shine again, and someday the benefits of love will overcome the benefits of remaining alone. Divorce has benefits, and it really is not the end of the world.

MECHELLE BROC

Birthday Girl

She wakes up early in the morning, thinking to herself, today is the day.

It's her sweet sixteenth birthday and no way would he let this one pass away.

You see, instead of enjoying the fantasies we see on MTV

And how they portray sweet sixteenth birthdays are supposed to be...

Babygirl hadn't enjoyed a birthday with her father since the age of three

Daddy claimed to be reality like T.V. does,

But he traded out the role of father for just every now and again hugs

To the public she seems fine, but deep in the back of her mind,

It's been killing her softly with time ...

Honestly thinking that this man could ever give two shrugs,

Whether she winds up on drugs

Or sliding the pole in somebody's club ...

And she hated how that after all this,

Her heart continued to show love for him.

And no matter how absent he had been,

She still felt that deep down somewhere there was love in him.

You see, father didn't vibe with mother anymore,

So he let his anger make him ignore the daughter that he used to adore.

She thinks back to the days when they would spend hours watching Disney videos

And how they used to watch Martin together, yeah, every episode ...

But the plot to this one sitcom, like family is not episodic, nor ironic

Yet it's as common as a bartender here and a patron asking for a gin and tonic

Since daddy's absence,

Babygirl hits supersonic mode and quickly grows up ...

Yeah, her body matched the age she was trying to act

But Babygirl didn't allow time for her mind to catch up ...

So now she's out there in life stuck,

Not even knowing which way is up.

Babygirl, if you just chill and listen....

I'm trying to tell you what's up.

See, there is so much more in store for you than to let this BS you adore control you

Yeah, I can open the door and show you the way,

But I can't walk through it for you ...

But if you get your soul together,

I guarantee your body will follow through.

And maybe then you will start to realize ...

That your true power lies right in between your eyes ...

And I never thought you were special just because of what was in between your thighs.

So not only do I understand, but Babygirl I empathize with you ...

And if I could give you the answers to life's questions,

Babygirl, I'd give them to you.

But for now, I just need to you trust and believe in yourself,

Pick yourself up ...

Gather yourself together ...

And if needed, go get yourself some help.

See, daddy's issues are no longer yours to bear,

That dude left you behind … So, therefore, leave those issues there.

So now in your moments of weaknesses and missed birthdays,

No longer do you have to cry …

Just remember your purpose for being here,

Keep your head towards the sky,

No lie girl …

You made it this far and I'm proud of you

And if that man doesn't ever tell you again,

Babygirl, I will tell you …

Happy Birthday

JoeP

Single-Parent Households

In the United States, 22 million children go home to one parent, and 83 percent of those parents are moms. A single-mother home is much more common than a single-father home; however, the number of single fathers has grown by 60% in the last ten years alone. It has been found that of all custodial parents, 82.2% were mothers and 17.8% were fathers (U.S. Census Bureau). Also, half of all children involved in one-parent households headed by the mother do not see their fathers on a regular basis two years after the breakup of the family (Grall, 2011). It has been found through varied research that children in single-parent homes generally fare worse than those in homes with two parents. Statistically, in the United States, family structure does contribute to certain characteristics of a child's well-being. Also, the number of children ages 15-17 in school and in good health is much lower in this group of children, and the number of children becoming pregnant at these ages is increasing. Problems found in the single-parent household may not be because of the parent who raised these children, but can be linked to other things that are also related to single parenting. It has been pointed out that when there is only one parent, the family is often less well off financially and this is the main reason for so many family problems. Reports show that the effects of coming from a low-income family can include things like lower education levels and lower economic achievement and can result in leaving the child feeling isolated and lonely. Being a single parent and struggling for money often coincide. It is also true that children of one-parent households are generally less supervised, their actions are less monitored and there is usually less communication between the child and parent. It would appear that being a part of a single-parent household indicates a negative family environment. It should be said, however, that many single-parent families find a balance and successfully thrive in today's world.

Single-Mother Households

It has already been stated that single-mother households are the most common type of one-parent family. Single mothers face different challenges from single fathers. Approximately seventy percent of single-parent mothers live in poverty, earning less than $13,000 annually. These women have a harder time providing for their families because they generally have lower paying jobs. Single mothers have all of the problems that lower income families have, with the added responsibility of raising a child on top of it. Even though women face greater financial problems, they tend to be more nurturing to their children by telling them they love them, hugging them, and showing affection towards them. Some positive aspects that may be associated with being a single mother are that, as opposed to males, they usually have a more extensive support system. Women are often closer to friends and family who can help them through tough times and even be there to support the mother in raising her children. The negative aspects of single-motherhood are that because women make less money, they have to work longer hours, which leaves them with less time for the children.

A single woman has to have the strength and the courage to not only be a mother but at times a father to her child(ren). You have to have the mental ability to make decisions as both parents would, all while keeping the child's or children's best interest at heart. We make it look so easy but are often criticized when we are more than likely doing our best. Most men would say that a woman couldn't teach a boy how to be a man. And the truth is …. we can't! But the fact is that a lot of them won't man up and do it, so we do our best. And I believe that GOD rewards us with a sixth sense to do so. It's no easy job and you've got to take the good along with the bad.

Child support does not make up for a father spending time with his child. And most of the time, the child support is not even enough to support the child nor does it begin to make up for the time that the father doesn't spend with the child. Often, he thinks that he is hurting the mother by not being responsible, but he is only hurting the child as well as himself. Time is one thing that you can't get back; children grow up and they remember. The sad thing is that at some point the father will want to be bothered with the child but will end up getting the same rejection that he once gave. I think that once the father digests and understands that, he will change his actions as well as his way of thinking. Another thing that affects the child is when the father makes promises to the child that he doesn't plan to or can't keep.

The mother then has to deal with the repercussions, which is usually a crying child that has to be comforted because daddy didn't come through yet again. That is major and can change the relationship tremendously. My solution to this is to make sure the father only tells you the plans he has versus telling the child. Until he calls and confirms the plans, the child doesn't have to know. That way everyone is happy and dad is not left looking like a liar.

Being a single mother with kids is a hard enough job within itself, but add dating to the equation and it gets even harder! Balancing the two requires much strategy. At times it gets lonely just giving all of yourself to the child(ren). Sometimes we want to receive that same love and affection that we are constantly showing and giving. But you have to be careful when dating. Not everyone deserves to be brought home to meet the child(ren). As a mother, you want to always remain the apple of your child(ren)'s eyes. But once you introduce the two, you have to start dividing your time and being careful not to offend anyone. Be creative. Children, especially boys (as in my case), are not so welcoming to another man being around their mom when they are used to having her to themselves. It creates tension and will sometimes put a strain on both relationships. The key is to make sure they get to know each other by allowing the child and the companion to spend alone time, then everyone together, and finally some one-on-one time between mates.

Single motherhood is a job that I wouldn't trade for the world. It has brought me so much joy. There is no greater gift than to be trusted enough by GOD for HIM to use you to carry and raise one of his own. On my saddest days my son has the ability to make it all better with one silly face, a joke, a kind word, or simply by telling me how much he loves me. GOD will never bring you to anything that HE doesn't plan to bring you through. I have shed tears of joy as well as tears of pain. Tears of joy have come at the thought of me having the ability to have a child, a healthy child at that. It is definitely GOD'S gift to women, and one that he doesn't reward every woman with. I am grateful that HE chose me. I get teary-eyed just looking at him growing up right in front of my eyes, so precious. But along with the tears of joy come the tears of pain. I cry at the thought of knowing that I have to do this alone. But I also know that if GOD brings me to it, HE will bring me through it. There is also a lot of anger involved. But, after the tears and anger come laughter and love in which we share a great deal.

Despite it all, it is a blessing and the situation in itself has built character and has strengthened me. The mere fact that I am able to do/have all that I have for us is a blessing within itself. It is no easy task, but through prayer and obedience to GOD it and everything else is totally possible. I have created a life that I think my son would be totally proud of. I try to live my life as a role model for him and try my best to teach him the ropes of life. And although statistics prove that if a child grows up in a single-family household they are more likely to end up in one, I don't want that to be the case with my son. I want him to be totally involved in the life of his children as well as [his] wife [and mother] of his children.

Getting a full night's rest is almost impossible these days. You have to get up early in the morning to make sure that all is well after being up all night getting things together for the next morning.

Effective planning, decision-making, and budgeting can relieve some of the struggles we face. If you plan things effectively, you can accomplish things better. Establishing a weekly schedule helps to keep things in balance. Decision-making is another thing that can help out with making things easier. Creating a budget can also help keep things in perspective.

Keeping your sanity in the midst of it all requires complete focus. Going to church helps me to maintain my sanity as well as to focus. Prayer changes things.

Working together with the father and deciding to make things work in spite of makes it so much easier for the child. In my situation I have just decided that because I did not make this child by myself, I am not going to raise him by myself even though his father does not live in the home with us. I will not let him off the hook that easily. And I'm not talking financially. I just don't believe in letting the father run footloose and fancy free while I'm stuck raising the child. I think that he should have just as much responsibility time wise as I do. I used to rush to go pick my son up right after work when he's with his dad but now I don't. I take care of whatever it is that I need to do first, including taking a nap if need be, before I pick him up. I used to feel guilty but he is not the only person with things to do. And I'm tired of paying people to watch my son when he has a dad who is in good health that can do it for me. In the long run, as angry as it sometimes makes his father, I think that he will appreciate me. Again, you can't get time back and you can't go back and redo the things you should have.

On the flip side, you have mothers who don't make the situation any easier because they use the child against the father, as well as what they get/don't get from him against him. If they get what they want then they are fine, but if not, all hell breaks loose! That is something else the child will grow up and remember. They get older and realize that the mother's so called reasoning behind keeping the child and father apart was a lie. I personally am not the type of mother who will use her child against the father. GOD put this child in ME, so it will be ME who will sacrifice all that I have and am to ensure that I have and will continue to provide for and support him. He comes first to me no matter what because he didn't ask to be here. What his dad does or doesn't do is his business; he receives no pressure from me financially. However, I still try to make sure that he gets to spend time with him.

There are 1.4 million single-parent run households. That alone is absolutely amazing to me. There are enough of us to come together and orchestrate something great. We should all stick together; a support system is definitely needed. I think that there are a lot of tips that we can give to each other to make life easier for all involved; we can also share experiences that we've been through. I think that most of us need to know that we are not alone in this.

Stephanie Hines

Mother Earth, Mother Nature, Mother

First and foremost, this is not an attack but instead some tough love. Life can be difficult sometimes. The management of life in general – going to work, balancing monetary obligations, a household (married or single), raising children, social interaction and relationships – can be overwhelming. This juggling act to balance everything can be quite stressful if you do not know how to position yourself for success. Do you have a set of morals and values? Do you have a standard that you are willing to uphold by your virtue? Do you have a goal?

Were you forced into womanhood because of the responsibility you have been entrusted with? Or was your forced womanhood a tradeoff for the irresponsible decisions you have made? Whatever your question and whatever your answer is, take time to access it, answer it, and address it. You must keep yourself evolving. And we know you are tired. Press on! Life is filled with trying challenges day in and day out. Out of all the challenges, you must remember one: Without you, we will fail. You are the resuscitating breath that refreshes life time and time again. The one thing that you must realize is that while you exist, others need you to exist. Life is more than a sunrise and sunset and everything that is happening in between. Life is about believing. Life is about making circumstances better for yourself and those around you. Life is about the "push", the determination, the tenacity to fight for a better day. Did you know making those around you better actually starts with you? Leadership by way of being the best you can be is the building block for a solid family foundation (single or married). You may not realize it, but you are the key to life. If you fail, we all fail. And you should know that a woman lost is a nation lost. We cannot do it without you. You have to be on point and it starts with self-awareness and rational thinking.

Rate Yourself As a Parent: Are You a Disengaged Parent?

Parents, your children are a reflection of you. It is your responsibility if your child is lying, stealing cheating, smoking, drinking, fornicating, or following in your footsteps in making irrational decisions. It is their action but it is still your responsibility, no matter how old they get. It's not your fault, but you may be the blame and you take accountability for it if it is – period, point blank. The apple does not fall far from the tree. Their actions can always be mirrored in what you did or did not provide. Parents are surprised when they find their children going astray. If they really drilled down past the symptom and got to the root, "surprised" would not apply. Maybe it was inevitable or it was just a matter of time. Then here it comes, the famous question, "Where did I go wrong?" Let me tell you: You went wrong when you took a break from parenting and didn't come back. Parents do not do enough these days. Is parenting really that hard or are your babysitters Xbox, Facebook, and TV providing the morals?

Do you expect your child to understand your rights and their wrongs (which are ultimately your wrongs), when there is the theory of eight: 8 hours of school, 8 hours of TV and video games, and 8 hours of sleep. You may be at work (I applaud you) you may be at home (I know it's a job finding a job), but you are the key and if you don't get it together our kids will grow up to fail. How much time did you with your child today (during the week)?

Look at it like this: 5*24 =120 hours (5 days in the week). You have the weekends 2*24= 48 hours. Can you effectively raise your children looking at 120 of business hours vs. maybe 48 hours of quality time (that is, if you actually sit down and instill some life and cognitive skills, life lessons, and information dissemination).

Monday through Friday Breakdown:

- 40 hours of the teachers and the streets raising your children
- 40 hours of sleep
- 15 hours of PlayStation and TV
- 10 hours of hygiene (morning and evening)
- 5 hours to eat dinner
- 10 hours of unsupervised homework

It's time for a drastic change. Stop being your child's buddy or friend. Be a parent. It takes more than asking "how was school today?" It takes more than punishment. It takes more than "good job, keep up the good work." It takes time, patience, and knowing that together we all can be successful in influencing our children's behavior.

It takes a village and sometimes you have to realize that you are the village ... the mother ... father ... uncle ... aunt ... and even Madea. Take responsibility for your situation and be successful. Is it hard as hell? Yes, but remember nothing worth having comes easy nor is realized without some type of sacrifice. Our future lies in our decisions. Bad decisions are like time ... once we make them, we cannot get them back. We can try hard to reverse them, but trying to reverse them is never as good as making the right decision the first time. The right decision the first time is to invest in ourselves as parents so we can be the best examples we can be for our children. Investing in your future means investing in your children's future; there is no separation. Your children see you and will follow suit to invest in themselves. And vice versa ... they see you lying, cheating, stealing, and taking advantage of others ... trust they will have insight and an example to do the same.

Someone did not just come up with the phrase "the apple doesn't fall far from the tree" for no reason. At any rate, let's realize that our future depends on our children and how we raise them. Love them ... discipline them ... then love them again. This may not work for everyone but find your way to be successful in raising your own. Society did not have those children and we have come far from a time where it is society's responsibility to raise them. Hopefully this inspires somebody to reassess their situation and do a better job. Hopefully this reached you and we do not have to wait until it's too late and you finally get it after listening to you and your child become the sad headline of the hour on the news at 10:00.

Single mothers and fathers: There are plenty of FREE resources in your area. Make sure to reach out to Big Brothers and Sisters, the YMCA and the YWCA, local city government, and your local church. Help is usually just a phone call away.

The future of life will depend on another trilogy. The trilogy of woman, family, and society. The trilogy that starts with woman.

A woman must embrace, define, and establish herself = Self-worth.

Once she has established her self–worth, she must use this strength to guide her family (husband and children). Women supporting their husbands or themselves and raising children who are productive members of society is the vision.

Society functions better as a whole when family units are productive. This unit gives inspiration and reflects abundant love, unity, communication, and resiliency in a family which is influenced by action of a strong, God-fearing woman.

Family: In the spring of 2010, an estimated 13.7 million parents had custody of 22 million children under 21 years of age while the other parent lived somewhere else. The family dynamic is different and must be addressed as such. Recognize that 82.2% of single-parent households are run by women; this is a red flag to society that there is an opportunity with family. This is a chain that has to be broken. This is real-time reality.

The UNBALANCE

A dysfunctional mother and father (married couple) raised a dysfunctional child. This dysfunctional child becomes a dysfunctional adult.

This dysfunctional adult has her own child from a dysfunctional relationship. Dysfunctional parents who have not addressed their dysfunctional ways will raise another dysfunctional child; this chain was not created on purpose. This chain was created out of ignorance and circumstance. The adults and children in this situation are only conforming to their mental and emotional skill sets.

The chain of dysfunctional children evolving into dysfunctional parents and adults passing their dysfunctional traits along has to stop. The chain can be broken. Realizing options and your worth is the key. Accepting and adjusting to the dynamic is the future. You are the key, the future, the backbone and visionaries to life. The fruition of future excellence is you and now.

It Will Come to Pass

Virtue: Goodness, merit, and chastity are all examples of moral excellence. Being a young lady whose father was unavailable in my life, I longed for positive male validation in my family unit. The only male in my family I have strong memories of was my grandfather who was sharp with words and not in an encouraging way. There was no question that he loved me. I knew I was his favorite girl. He was an unfortunate product of where he came from and was a military man of World Wars I and II.

As a result, family dysfunction – along with a mix of chaotic and controlling family traits – became my example of what I should tolerate and not expect from men. My grandfather was very crass, meaning he lacked sensitivity or consideration when it came to others; and, in our home, it was his way or no way. He was my only example of a father figure, support system, boyfriend, and husband. I was doomed from the start because my grandmother and mother were caught in the cycle of accepting, settling, and believing that my grandfather would change or that the situation would get better. I would soon face the repercussions of their misjudgments through the misjudgments of my own.

We are impressionable beings when we grace this earth and we live, breathe, and expand our character through the family that God blesses you with. These people – good, bad or indifferent – are the foundation and the influence on how we interact with the world. Home and the family structure are where our moral fiber is perfectly guided or imperfectly misguided. Unfortunately, home was the place where the beginnings of my precious pretties were ravished.

A recipient of these imperfectly misguided circumstances left me looking for male affirmation in all the wrong places early in life. I was desperate for attention. I was also naive when it came to meeting people and having a good ability of discerning their character ... you know, the representative they send before they show you the real them. As I look back it seems foolish, but when he told me he had been to jail and had just come home, I was drawn in instead of deterred. My naivety, intrigue, and his charisma were a concoction for disaster. Instead of running in the opposite direction, I was whispering sweet nothings until the wee hours of the morning. Our friendship and interaction were mostly on the phone and through Facebook. As things progressed, I had the opportunity of visiting with him at his home. His mother kept a close eye on us, but we still managed to do what teenagers do. Up to this point the only physical contact we had were a few hugs and some kisses.

He was a bad influence but he was also my confirmation to what I thought was womanhood. Full of myself, my eyes were wide shut and my legs and nose wide open. More TNT was added to the already volatile concoction and I was literally ready to explode. The opportunity came where the fuse was lit and the explosion would change my life forever.

A summer night, a summer dress, and a summer party were the agenda and the atmosphere. A few friends were getting together to mix and mingle. This was where I had my first taste of alcohol; a few sips and you could not tell me anything. I received a call from my friend; his timing was great. He wanted to come and take me for a ride. I figured I'm already out at a party; I'll just step away with him for a little bit and no one will even notice.

When he arrived, he had a friend with him. I was hesitant to go but something was in the air ... or my drink made me feel like so. I got in and we drove to a park. We got out of the car and began to walk through the park. We were talking while he and his friend were playing like friends do. We walked for about five minutes before we saw a table and sat down. His friend stayed off in the distance talking on his phone.

He began to kiss and touch me all over. It felt good but even in my tipsy state I knew the park table was not the ambiance I wanted for this type of foreplay. I began to refuse his advances and he lost it. I became every bitch and hoe that I had only witnessed other people being called. Everything happened so fast. His friend was off of the phone and joining in. How his distance shrunk had me in awe. He grabbed my arms and his friend grabbed my mouth; I will never forget thinking what I did to get myself in this position. I kicked and bit and was finally able to scream. My spirit of not wanting to be a rape statistic was stronger than their will to rape me. Kicking, screaming, and squirming became too much for them to control and they let me go and began to run to the car. Shirt half ripped, I grabbed my breath and began to run the opposite way. Shocked and hysterical, I ran in the dark using little glimmers of light to guide my way through the trail. Scared to death that they would circle back for me, I paused. The scene was quiet. The moon, the stars, and my fear. I still felt as someone was looking at me. Five minutes of contemplating whether to go or not felt like an hour. I got up and continued to follow the glimmers and finally made my way to a path that led to a park exit. I tried to flag a few cars down but no one stopped. I continued to walk along the streets in daze until I made it to a corner store where I called police. They took me home. I was physically and mentally dirty and scratched up and in a shameful daze when I got out of the patrol car. Doors and windows to my apartment building were opening up. People wanted to see what was going on. My mother was one of those people until she realized it was me. The questions began to flow. She wanted answers. Feeling stupid and victimized, as though I deserved what just happened to me, all I could say was nothing over and over. Was it truly my fault or did they take advantage of my naivety and vulnerability?

I do not know what felt worse. The fact that I felt worthless or the fact that the ordeal I had gone through could have been avoided. You always think you know better until that moment of knowing better comes. Compartmentalizing more hurt, shame and physical pain my virtue becoming my vice. (Vice is a practice or a behavior or a habit considered immoral, depraved or degrading in the associated society.) In minor usage, vice can refer to a fault, a defect, an infirmity or merely a bad habit.

I think my bad habit was my upbringing. It's funny, but not having a father hurts me more than I can appreciate having a mother that cares, I guess. When you have feelings of worthlessness, value of being less than and have no standards or moral compass to guide you, you attract people that have some of the same traits, family structure or even the lack thereof.

The aftermath of this is that I have dealt with the effect of an absent father. My mother has acknowledged her role in my bad choices. She has since tried to help me by starting the eye-opening process of dealing with her issues of my dad abandoning us and their relationship. By ignoring her feelings, she unknowingly passed on her trait of denial which ultimately affected how I processed my own feelings.

We both agreed that establishing a relationship with God and one another is where healing and renewed life begins. Through this lesson, we are both embracing the faith of a mustard seed and we are both growing in discernment in our decisions. We know that healing and understanding will not be complete today or tomorrow, but we have forgiven and accepted that it will come. I did not want to but, after I realized that this incident was not my fault, I pressed charges. It was my duty to at least try to see that this did not happen to anyone else. He, his friend, and the vehicle were all placed at the scene. They both were looking at serious time because they had prior offenses. Ironically, his friend testified on my behalf to receive leniency in sentencing. Life is crazy when you peek at it but, once you take a good long stare at it, it all makes sense. They both are serving time. God is good.

Tangela Russ

Women are creatures of emotion, so it is difficult to pry the emotions of love, loneliness, pain, betrayal, forgiveness, and many other challenging anxieties from the tight grips of their mentality. The education, resources, and coping skills are not getting disseminated adequately to the female population whether it is from grandmother to mother, mother to daughter, or sister to sister. And there are people embarrassed to receive them because of how people judge them. We (everyone who desires a better society) have to educate and find viable avenues to discuss and address fears and challenges that females face.

This book will present 9 avenues that have been around for ages but never presented in such a way. These avenues can help everyone from the richest of the rich to the poorest of the poor.

Woman

A woman is a multi-faceted creature, the epitome of strength in times when no one else can cope. A woman can produce, provide, prevent, console, and bring wholeness through the nurturing of her hands and the wisdom from her lips.

The firmness of her backbone and the toughness of her skin can endure a trial that seems impossible to the mightiest of beings.

You may wonder how it is that I can speak so majestically about a woman, and I can tell you that I am the woman who is the epitome of strength by upholding my husband when he is in a trial that seems only God can fix. I give him the very essence of me which encompasses an unexplainable connection. I am one that can produce life that brings joy to the world through his smile and footsteps through the earth. I provide and contribute my wisdom and effervescent joy to my surroundings. I console those that are in need of sound and unbiased advice when there is no other shoulder to lean on.

My hands and my very presence can create an atmosphere that will soften a stony heart. My tough skin allows me to be a professional, career-driven being, without breaking down when I am overlooked for a promotion, or disliked and demeaned because of my beauty-stricken outer appearance. I refuse to scale down my attire to compromise my self-esteem by disrespecting my constituents and higher-ups. I must remain true to myself and, if I constantly change to make others happy, I would be a hypocrite.

I must continue to strive for perfection. I owe all of my strength and talents to the One who anoints my head from on high every morning so that I may grace society with my presence, and leave a special thought of what a woman is in the minds of those with whom I come in direct contact.

I place myself under strict scrutiny to always be mindful that my life as a woman can always be improved. This is a never-ending journey that I must press my way through. If there is ever a time that I feel I am not shining through as the light that was placed within me, I revisit in my mind all the times that I have placed a smile on a face or nursed an inner wound back to esteem.

I am a multi-faceted creature.

I am a more than a rib.

Deonna Benton

Perspective, Healing, Empowerment

The world is a crazy place. Most of us are born into our circumstance. As a child, it is up to the caretakers that we have been entrusted with to care for our well-being. Over time, those people can feel lost, become burdened, corrupted, bound and stressed as a result of balancing and managing their everyday lives.

In the midst of the balancing act, the stress of life forces drastic and inappropriate actions that can present itself in the form of rape, domestic violence, adultery, and divorce.

These ugly actions and consequences are having devastating effects on the victims these crimes are being perpetrated against. The victims are the most vulnerable ... children, teenagers, followers, those with low self-esteem and who do not know their value and worth.

We are born into times and circumstance; and this book's purpose is to educate past, present, and future societies on balancing life in order to make effective decisions.

The transformation starts with you, and by default will impact your family and society as a whole.

There is an overwhelming amount of statistics that point to women as being victims of domestic violence, rape, and divorce. We will concentrate on the education of women as there is a demand for it, as well as instruction in order to promote advocating success, and proactive measures to stay healthy both mentally and physically. We will also focus on healing, empowerment and perspective in addition to achieving forgiveness once enlightenment through our thought processes is achieved.

Part II: Perspective

Perspective Comes with Honest and Clarity

Pillar #1

Self-Assessment

Rather than love, than money, than fame, give me truth.

Thoreau

- Self-acceptance is the first step in realizing the power of control. Getting back to self will start to reveal clarity and blessings in many different layers.
- One might even begin to feel guilty as you begin to explore yourself and focus on bettering you. Please do not feel guilty for getting back to self because you are going to have to let go of some things.
- Just remember that you will not be able to truly interact and function effectively, successfully, and abundantly with others and self until this transition into the new you is complete.
- Getting back to self is getting back to God. You should be realizing that this relationship is paramount in the new you.

The only time I don't see who is in the mirror is when I'm not true with myself.

When is the last time that you have talked to yourself? You are not crazy to do so although others in your circle may question you. But is it not a crazier situation that you would weigh the thoughts and perception of others questioning or rationalizing you questioning yourself? See, this is the problem in the world. We are looking for others' approval versus approval from ourselves and our situations. We will often take advice from illusion artists: You know, people that have the Lexus or Mercedes Benz and the sky rise or house on the hill but really cannot afford it and are living check to check, or marriage and children in turmoil, or a plain façade that is immaculately presented. You know presentation is all in perception. You can bring lobster and steak on a platter with all the fixings and you will feast. You bring that same lobster and steal on a trash can lid and the presentation will change your perception.

We must accept ourselves and our situation for what we and they are. We must accept, realize and decide whether we are going to make a change or not. There is nothing wrong with being content. There is nothing wrong with striving for greatness. But you are and have been at that fork in the road and it's time to make a decision. Now is the time. Not tomorrow, not on the next Jane life class, right now ... write your check and cash it.

Shape Shifters

By definition, shape shifting occurs when someone either has the ability to change their shape into that of another person or entity, or finds its shape involuntarily changed by someone else.

In my case, the latter definition applied to me. Shape shifting occurred in three trusted areas of my life. Here is what shaped anger inside of me:

1) My BFF of twenty years slept with my husband. She was that problem-solving, soup-bringing, I'm-here-if-you-need-me friend with big ears and a heart to match. (Or so I thought!)

I trusted her with my money, my man, and my child. I invited her into areas of my life that no one else knew of.

I buried my guards into our friendship. I did not think I needed them with her. Man, was I wrong! The thought of her betraying me never crossed my mind. I was a true friend to her. I gave with no expectations; I listened to her 3:00 am cries without passing judgment. I was the one that encouraged her to tear down barriers in her life. I built her up when other people tore her down.

I welcomed her into my life, my world, my home. What on earth was I thinking? Don't get me wrong, I'm not dismissing his role in this; but I think I could have handled it better if it was anyone else but her. It broke my heart as well as my spirit.

Who was I going to talk to about this? She was my empathetic sister whenever things went wrong. In an instant, we both lost our best friend.

When my heart paused to evict her, I felt my soul crumble. I was too weak to stand up to this stranger I had known for twenty years.

She left me in a dilapidated state. I had no choice but to hate her. She shaped her best friend into her worst enemy.

2) I am in the small percentage of people who thinks that people of the opposite sex can maintain a close, strictly platonic relationship. Nick and I met through a mutual friend. We hit it off immediately. Nick was exceptionally handsome; but he was not my type. I made it clear to him, early on, that I only wanted to be friends.

He was okay with that, so I felt comfortable around him. We shared a lot of our personal lives with each other. We hung out so much that it was hard to convince people that we were not a couple.

I set him up on a few dates, but for some reason, none of them worked out. His favorite line to me was, "You need to show them what a real woman is."

I did not read too much into it because Nick was my friend and we had an understanding.

Well, to make a long story short … Nick became buddies with the guy I was dating at the time, which I thought was cool even though I did not get to spend much time with either of them.

Two months later, my dude and I split up. Afterwards, Nick and I went back to our old routine of chilling with each other regularly. Eventually he cut all ties with my ex. During one of our conversations, he rambled about how much I meant to him and that my ex did not deserve a woman like me and so on and so forth. Then, he revealed that he had secretly been in love with me for quite some time and he had motives of befriending my ex. He told me about the lies and manipulation he used to persuade old dude to cheat on me.

Nick knew about the situation with my ex-husband and my friend. I could not believe he was a part of this betrayal.

He swore that it was for my own good. He thought that we could move forward from this point. Nick was wrong! I left him in the shadows of his thoughts, broken and alone while I stood on the edge of sadness.

His shift was over! How could we shape a relationship based on lies?

3) My breach in faith. I was the "good girl" type. I had a strong spiritual side, so I was very active in the church. I took pride in my education and carried myself in a respectable manner. I only dated guys whom I felt were compatible with me and who would be accepted by my family and friends.

So, the thug/hood guy would never work. But, there was something about them that I was so attracted to. Needless to say, my relationship was not going well with my so-called compatible mates.

This led me to stray from the norm and I became involved with the thug of all thugs. This intelligent, bad boy exposed me to a very sexy, chaotic world.

He put me in dangerous situations, but made up for it by satisfying my materialistic side. He also had no problems expressing his love for me. I knew in my heart that what I was doing was wrong but, I was in love with knowing that a person like him, who did not care about anything or anybody, could love me so much.

I was the only one that could penetrate his hard exterior. I assumed God was not blessing the relationships that I thought I was supposed to be in, so why not try something different.

My idiosyncratic behavior quickly became too much for my friends and family to handle so I made the decision to cut them out of my life. In the process of doing that, I also severed my spiritual ties with God.

I stopped going to church because it was cutting into the time that I spent with him. After transforming from his trophy piece to his punching bag, I realized that he had changed me into the opposite of myself.

I did not know whether to blame God for allowing me to go through such a horrible ordeal or blame the devil for making it so attractive.

My spirit was slumped over inside the bruised casings of a faithless woman. I was a stranger to myself. I was in no shape to even pray.

During a momentary breach of security, Satan slipped through a hairline crack in my spirit. I gave him a piece of my soul in return for my soul's peace. But in my greatest time of need, God stood up in my daughter's smile, because He knew that it was the only thing I was holding on to. I knew then, there was still hope. So, I pulled the pieces of me towards the center of which I am and experienced wholeness once again. I felt complete and anxious to move forward. I realized that no task was greater than my strength. Here are my footsteps on the path to reshaping this person that was crouched inside of me:

Out of chaos emerged creation, the creation of a beautiful, strong, determined woman of purpose.

I was bruised but not broken; I stumbled but did not fall.

My undying faith enabled me to move mountains and soar beyond the midst of my adversities.

You see, my life was never a bed of roses.

I took what was inflicted upon me into the outside world ... wore it like a cloak of knowledge.

Experience was my dagger.

I felt that I had endured all possible hurt from within the walls of my dungeon in which I dwelled.

With invincible thoughts, I was ready to face the world ...

Outside of my familiar zone, my task was to unveil and identify my friends and foes.

It was sometimes hard to tell the difference between the two, even without the mask.

I laid down my sword and shield to love.

Only to have to pick them back up to protect myself from the iron blows of the one who professed to love me.

Yet, I did not lose my head. I gained focus.

I dodged the bullets of drugs and alcohol that could have impaired my thoughts and sealed my doom. I have seen women in these positions fall victim to the enemy of destruction.

With adversity on every hand, I was steadfast in my belief.

I stood when there was no support. I shaped myself from the inside out.

I knew that I had a choice to either be crippled by my conditions or use them as tools of wisdom and strength. So, I chose the latter.

I had to identify my worth and step to myself correctly so that others would know how to step to me.

I had to confront myself to confirm myself.

I looked beyond my circumstances and saw a glimmer of light that aligned my footsteps and shifted my path toward the shape of redemption.

I am ahead of myself in this race! Now, I'm just waiting on time to catch up with purpose. I am shaped to shift defeat.

When levees are ruptured, trying to follow the beat of your blood can be difficult.

Your flow gets clotted with confusion and distrust. You lose faith in yourself and everyone around you.

Order your spirit to stand up!

Shift the shape of your storm so that it is easily weathered.

Shape Shifters! Solidarity starts from within.

Man cannot restructure what God has built.

Sharon Young

Reflections of Truth

On the outside I was beautiful. I was 5'6" with rollercoaster curves, flawless midnight skin, with a pretty smile. On the inside I was a hot mess.

As I stared at myself in the mirror, I could hear my mother's voice, "If you cannot be honest with yourself, you will not be able to be honest with anyone." I laugh as I said it out loud, "I guess I am the world's biggest liar because I have been lying to myself for years." It took the harsh, but loving, words of my best friend Maya to make me realize that I was like this because of my own unhappiness and drama.

I played a major part in my failed relationships, broken dreams, and distorted self-image. I could no longer place all the blame on someone else. It was all me; I was the common dominator.

I was taking Maya's advice. She suggested I take a long look in the mirror and reevaluate my life and discover the root of why I was so unhappy.

I needed to do an honest and brutal self-assessment, a true reality check. I stood in the mirror for hours staring at my own reflection listing my grievances, praying, crying, and whining, mostly of how everyone had done me so wrong.

I was having a pity party. After it was done and over with, I began reflecting and suddenly things became so clear.

123

Like most women, I dreamed of getting married, but I knew if I continued down this path, that dream would never happen.

I was finally digesting my role in my failed relationships. I need to take time to discover myself and fall in love with me.

I had spent so many years of picking the wrong men because I did not know my own self-worth. Anytime a guy showed me any kind of attention, I was immediately drawn to him, even if the attention was negative.

Not knowing my own value led me to settle for men that did not want to be in a committed relationship. The majority of them were open and honest about their feelings, but I refused to listen and devoted myself to anyone who did not want to be with me long term.

I thought if I showed them how wonderful and giving I could be, eventually they would give in. I became trapped in the cycle of giving myself away and receiving nothing in return. Once they grew tired of me sexually and my endless demands of wanting more, they walked away leaving me bitter and jaded.

Not only was my love life in disarray, so was my relationship with my mother. My mother and I were constantly in some type of battle with each other. I blamed her for all the unhappiness I experienced in my childhood and my insecurities.

I grew up in a single-parent home. My mother struggled to provide for me and my sister. She was constantly working, sometimes two to three jobs at a time, which left little time for my sister and me.

I was starved for attention and affection. Now, years later, my mom was trying desperately to make up for what I longed for in my childhood – but I refused to let the past go.

I sabotaged any attempts or plans that she made for us to become closer, because I had not forgiven her for past hurts. I was now realizing I was having such a hard time forgiving her because I could not forgive myself.

I could not forgive myself for all the things I had done when I was seeking out the attention and affection of men that I was not getting at home.

I was a wild teen; I did everything from skipping school, shoplifting, experimenting with drugs, and being promiscuous. My wild ways led to an unwanted teen pregnancy that I kept a secret.

I terminated the pregnancy, but I was still very haunted by my decision. I was filled with so much remorse and guilt. I had been living with the guilt for over ten years.

I think it was time for me to discuss this issue with a professional so I could deal with my feelings and my issues of forgiveness.

My professional life was also a huge disappointment. I hated my job; it was boring and left me feeling drained and unsatisfied. I worked as a customer service rep for a financial company. I was verbally abused for nine hours a day. I constantly complained about how I hated my job and my supervisor. Sometimes I would sit in the parking lot before work and cry. I would pray that God would remove me from the situation, but faith without works is dead.

With all the whining and complaining I did, I never once made an effort to apply for other jobs. I was content in being unhappy.

In the words of Sam Cooke, a change was definitely going to come. I was finally going to take control of the things I could control.

Tomorrow morning I am calling in to work and spending my day at the local community college registering for business and fashion design classes.

As a little girl I used to dream of owning a boutique with my own clothing line. I was now going to turn that dream into a reality. I was making a promise to myself to create my own happiness and stop depending on others to bring me happiness.

I look at my reflection now and smile. I am finally beginning to love what I see reflecting back at me.

Contrina Jenkins

I GOT UP

I GOT UP AND SAID THIS TIME I'M GOING TO DO IT. I'M GOING TO PUT PEN TO PAPER AND I'M ACTUALLY GOING TO FOLLOW THROUGH THIS TIME. ONE SENTENCE TURNED INTO A PARAGRAPH ONE PARAGRAPH TURNED INTO A PLAN. ONE plan TURNED INTO A GOAL and HERE I AM PREGNANT AGAIN (Damn). Dream FULFILLED ON HOLD AGAIN. MY second CHILD WITH YET ANOTHER BABY DADDY. ANOTHER "I Promise TO BE THERE FOR YOU." ANOTHER TIME I made somebody a priority that labeled me as an option. I was burned out on putting others before myself. ANOTHER SATIFYING DISAPPOINT-MENT…. HOW DID I END UP LIKE THIS AGAIN? WELL, LET ME SEE.

I WAS SO IN LOVE THAT MY LOVE FOR HIM DERAILED ME FOR THE PLAN I HAD FOR MYSELF. 8 YEAR PLAN: BACHELORS, MASTERS, DOCTORATE. HOW DID INFATUATION AND A SMILE LEAD TO NINE POUNDS AND TEN OUNCES OF SINGLE RESPONSIBILITY? IN THE BLINK OF AN EYE IT BEGAN. DROPPING OUT OF COLLEGE STARTED WITH "I'M GOING TO TAKE SOME TIME OFF." I'M GOING TO TAKE SOME TIME OFF evolved INTO DAY CARE, A 9 TO 5, AND A ONE BEDROOM APARTMENT. HOW DID I BECOME NORMAL? THIS IS NOT THE LIFE I PLANNED FOR ME. I have become a statistic by living life with a plan but living life without condoms and commitment. I CANNOT TALK ABOUT IT LIKE LAST TIME I HAVE TO BE ABOUT IT. IT'S TIME TO GET BACK TO REALITY AND THE CHALLENGES AHEAD.

I am in my last stage of my pregnancy and don't know what to do. What AND WHO are my resources? What can I do to enlarge my territory? Let me pray.

God, all is not lost. Your blessing me with another life to be responsible for lets me know you have more in store for me. Give me clarity as I take the next necessary step in finding salvation and my purpose. In Jesus' name, Amen.

Prayer cancels out the pity party; now it's time to get focused. First thing in focusing I have to do is to start to love me and my kids first and unconditionally. I have been blessed in bringing forth life. My worth starts here. I must remain true to the purpose of my destiny. I am a queen. I was put on earth to govern life, reproduce, and help my partner with goals that help our family unit collectively. Since I have no partner (which many of us do not), I will live with an available, open, and focused vision. I must always take advantage of and be abreast of my surroundings and resources. This starts with educating myself.

In this education I must realize that I don't revolve around men; men revolve around me. You would think that God is the only one who provides favor, but we as women somehow find favor in men. Men giving us time, money, sex, and a key which turns our clarity and discernment into unsure decisions and sucker for love states of mind. We start letting our vaginas and hearts make decisions.

I want to take this time to reclaim my mind, body, and soul. I have children to raise, a degree to finish, bills to pay, and life to live. To be successful in accomplishing these tasks, I must focus and remember the most important thing that I ... we so easily forget ... my worth and my position in my situation. I am the head, not the tail. I rebuke the devil. I am great and I will do great things with or without a man's time, money, favor. My God will be my man. I will date him and his infinite wisdom and lonely will be no more. I thought I needed a man's validation. I realized I did not when I saw the same validation that I craved manifesting doubt and confusion. Thanking God for the past, those days and nights are gone. Single, lonely, educated, and knowing better have transitioned into fabulously single with two beautiful children, determined, and available. Available for all of God's blessings and all of the hard work I have ahead of me. I am available to live life with clarity and no reservations. I am available to live life with a partner or without a partner. More importantly, I am available to live life with no regrets, making rational decisions for the future. I am available to play the best hand out of the cards that are dealt and make lemonade out of lemons. I am available for life.

From this day forward I will not make excuses for myself, nor will I make excuses for you. I will try to be my best and accept that you are who you are even if your best is your worst. The clarity in knowing and not making excuses for either one of us will help me to make the best decision for me, my children, and my future. I think I got "IT" now. With God's strength I will keep "IT' this time.

Pillar # 2

Self-Accountability

"We are accountable only to ourselves for what happens to us in our lives."

Mildred Newman

- One must realize present, past, and future thinking patterns that a person has can and will bind one to a condition of limited realization, growth, and acceptance of the new you.

- This conditioning will act as a barrier to the process of admittance.

- Do not be ashamed of the mistake ... be proud of the decision to make a change.

- Do not let denial hold you hostage.

- The road to infinite possibilities does not begin until you say I have an issue ... I want to address this issue ... and I NEED SOME HELP. In addressing your opportunity, you must find a way to have humility in overcoming and humor in understanding. Nothing is accomplished without a plan and that goes for having a plan to be accountable for self. Everything in holding yourself accountable should be taken seriously but not to the degree that it is stressful. It is okay to have a high expectation of yourself. Be S.M.A.R.T with goals and aspirations.

- Specific
- Measurable
- Attainable
- Reachable
- Time sensitive (trackable)

It is hard to hold yourself accountable but it is very necessary in growth to the new you. Having a strong sense of self-accountability is the foundation of realization and strategy as it relates to being a responsible and accountable individual. Accountability assists in the preparation of correcting or improving your situation (everyone's different yet the same). Self-accountability simply means you are holding yourself responsible for your successes and failures. You own your beliefs, actions, and influence of your aura. Yes, you influence those around you, regardless if the energy generated is positive or negative. You have an imprint in the world similar to a virtual footprint and you can influence your circumstance and the circumstances of others by being accountable. You have power and it starts in accountability of self.

Self-accountability demands a consistent and conscious scrutiny of your own values and morals. The core of your ethical existence affords your accountability to make difficult decisions in the heat of the moment. Decisions grounded in accountability will reward you with desired results. For example, you have received that 2:00 am call. You know what he wants. Instead of succumbing to the flesh, press on with your accountability in being respectful to self and tell him that tomorrow's time spent will be just as good as tonight and to enjoy himself. This can be painful but do not forget that pain is irrationality and weakness leaving the body. When you are accountable, you have to come face to face with integrity and define what it means to you.

Integrity (being true to yourself) in your accountability should trump emotions when being accountable to yourself or holding someone else accountable in how he interacts with or treats you. Never let accountability be driven by distress, panic, guilt or fear. On the flip side, do not let it be driven by happiness, pleasure, or expectations. Do not concede to one side or the other. Accountability walks a fine line and must be balanced. If you do not balance the two sides, you will find yourself facing a sliding scale of accountability and picking and choosing when and when not to be accountable. Non-management of the two sides will make for many difficult decisions and many undesired outcomes.

Self-accountability can be intimidating. Self-accountability can also be empowering and rewarding. Self-accountability means you are responsible for successes and failures. You and only you are responsible for your actions. Remember you can pick the actions in being accountable, but you cannot pick the consequences of your actions in being non-accountable.

Accountability is personal truth to the standards one needs to establish, follow, and revisit with updates and improvement on a regular basis. Life evolves and so should we.

A Beautiful Lesson

Lauren grew up a very headstrong young lady, quite like her own mother, but with a little extra. From the time she was fifteen, Lauren took charge of her life and knew exactly what she wanted for it. She never settled for mediocrity or anyone who embraced it. Her mother was a lawyer, so since she was twelve she wanted to be a judge.

She would see how hard her mother worked many nights to become what she wanted to be. In this process, her mother taught her many lessons throughout life. The most important was the one of self-accountability.

Lauren remembers vividly her mother telling her all the time, "Everyone and everything in this world can only merely hurt you;

it is only you that can seriously hurt yourself and stop your own progress!" Her mother would say this time and time again, and then end it by questioning if Lauren knew exactly what she meant. Lauren would always understandingly answer, "Yes, I get it, mom," in response.

Her mother deeply wanted her to know that she could not always go through life blaming others for this or that. Nor should she surrender to the circumstances of life.

In essence, Lauren's mother made it her life's mission to keep her daughter well prepared and focused. Her mother knew all too well about what happens when you are not accountable for yourself.

Lauren's mother, Diane, grew up just like her, very strong minded and focused. She also had hopes of being a judge, the first female judge in the state.

Everything was going as planned until life brought a new, outgoing, careless, and potentially dangerous man into her life. He knew all of the right things to say that not only captivated her attention, but kept it.

He introduced her to things she had never done and experiences she had never had. Diane was intrigued by the lure of the danger, his wit, and the thoughts of what this could eventually be. She was so focused on him that she forgot her own priorities.

He demanded so much of her when she was at an age where she was supposed to be growing into what she was called to be, a judge. The relationship became such a burden for her.

The burden was so heavy it threw her off of the path she was once so very focused on. Not to mention, right before her senior year of college, she found that this exciting experience of a fling had now turned into her being pregnant. At the delivery of the news, he was gone with the wind, never to be seen or heard from again.

Though they were serious, Diane never really knew much about him, so searching for him was not an option. The first few months she fell into a depression, angry about being pregnant and left to face the situation all alone.

Diane blamed her friends for not warning her enough and not keeping her away from a man like that. She blamed life for giving her these tragedies, and then started to blame God for ignoring her and throwing her to the side.

She felt like God had taken His hands off of her and forgotten all about her well-being. She blamed the condom for bursting. She blamed everyone and everything in the world, besides herself.

She never took a glance in the mirror. If she had for one moment, perhaps she would have seen her own life and role in things and gain insight on who she had become.

She never wanted to acknowledge her own mistakes through all of this. She did not want to see how careless she had been.

She did not want to see the truth.

Though stumbling blocks came her way, she went on to graduate and have her daughter, Lauren. She finished at the top of her class and went on to pass the bar, getting hired right away.

She relinquished her dream of becoming a judge to take care of her Lauren and made sure that she raised her right. She taught her about God and how to love herself first, before anybody. She taught her to read very well and made sure she was smart and could think on her own. Diane wanted to instill in Lauren everything she thought she had lost, teaching her that most important lesson, to always hold herself accountable for her own actions.

Today, Diane sits six rows back from the stage watching her daughter graduate from law school, at the top of her class. Lauren is now on a clear path to being a great lawyer and eventually a judge.

Lauren is focused more than ever, and thanks God and her mother on this day for blessing her at an early age, with a beautiful lesson.

Joe P

The Downfalls of Being Too Independent

Bolting upright from a peaceful moment of sleep, I found myself blindly investigating the source of my rude awakening. I heard nothing from the bunk bed above me where my younger brother slept. Had I heard anything at all? Had my sleep habits simply become accustomed to the explosive alarm clock that had started to steal my rest many a night?

I guess I have been restless for a very long time. Is that when I started becoming prematurely anxious about things that had not yet happened? When I began hoping for the best to really only be planning for the worst!

When I first began to realize how much you cannot depend on others, I made preparations to never have to do so. My stern shoulders lowered a bit as I cautiously lay back down and pulled the covers to my neck. Quiet surrounded me once again long enough for me to drift back into serenity.

"Not a bad night's rest," I thought when the morning sunlight tickled my eyelashes. I was still reveling in this thought when my Mama peeked her head into the room to get us up for school.

My heart fell into a cesspool of disappointment when I noticed the purple peeking over the top of her rose-tinted glasses. My z's were not interrupted in vain just hours before! Another black eye. Another morning of acting like nothing was wrong. Another morning of my skin crawling at the phony touch of my abusive stepfather. Hoping he would not start my day by cutting my fingernails down to the quick, AGAIN. As has been thus far the story of my life, I wondered why I had allowed myself to foolishly fantasize that a night had passed without event. I suppose that is where I began teaching myself that hoping would only lead to the disappointment of reality.

I eventually found myself expecting the worst and really just wanting to get it over with. Not even giving myself the chance for much of anything good.

Countless times a guy would catch my attention causing my heart to flutter only to be followed by the thought, "He would never go for me." I had been in survival mode for so long that I had very little experience with actual relationships; for the injuries that I was seeking to heal from were caused by relationships. I was not even ten years old when I vowed to myself that I would never have to depend on a man. Not so much that I had to accept being treated like garbage for my meals, or be degraded for the clothes on my back.

I may have had self-esteem issues but, thanks to my anger management struggles, I had my limits on the abuse that I would put up with. As time went on, I had yet become able to even imagine myself with a boyfriend or husband being that I had yet to see the benefits of one. Therefore, motherhood didn't much cross my mind either.

I figured that it was all just a part of life and we would all have to cross those rickety bridges eventually. I whimsically assumed that everyone eventually fell in love, eventually got married, and eventually had children.

I was going to get around to it. No need to rush.

I watched my Mama pack us up and leave a total of three times before it was for good. I remember the last women's shelter the clearest – partially because of my age, but I also think that the experiences and the people there left the deepest impressions on me.

The short order chef in the kitchen downstairs made the best grits in the world. They tasted like rainbows with melted butter. Quite vivid was the memory of the day we left that shelter. One of my first rare positive experiences with a male was that chef.

Every day after breakfast, he would allow us to dig through this extremely large box of toys in the kitchen. It was almost taller than me and held the most smiles I had ever seen at once.

From the very first awkward day that we spent there, I had my eyes on that four pack of play dough. Mama said, "Not a chance. You will just make a mess with that." After a few days I stopped asking, with my mouth anyways. Puppy dog eyes didn't work either.

Then came the day that it was time to leave and begin again. I begged this time. To my delight, she said, "We can't start over without a proper collection of play dough."

I can't forget Maryanne and her three girls. We could relate to them except it was me and my two brothers. Their father was about as friendly as my brothers' dad.

We all shared so much between us that we ended up leaving together. Our moms depended on each other to start their lives over. It was a two-bedroom duplex housing two adults and six kids, but it was so peaceful in comparison to what we had all been used to previously.

It really stuck with me, the tremendous effort it took my Mama to rebuild a better life for us as a single mother. I had no idea what I truly wanted out of life at this point, but I was pretty certain that I did not want to be a single mom.

Along the way, I also witnessed one of my aunts working full-time, dating, taking care of herself on her own and even having girls' nights out. This looked much more appealing to my barely budding female curiosity. Housewife and mother were too intertwined with a man.

Sure, there was no one else there to help bear the brunt of things such as bills, but if you knew that you could depend on yourself there was no need to worry. You weren't missing anything. I may have wanted someone but I didn't NEED anybody. I had worked very diligently to convince myself of that. My female guidance was very slim on substance.

My mother began to succumb to paranoid schizophrenia. My grandmother on her side did not speak. I do not know how else to explain that, but she just did not speak. That changed some after my repressive grandfather passed, but I still felt I had no hand to lead me from that direction.

The females on my dad's side tended to have negativity brewing and bubbling out of any available escapable crevice. Only so much progress can be reached when aiming to teach a child with your only weapon being negativity. There has to be some positive suggestions or examples to take that place.

Most of my friends in high school were teen moms before it was cool enough for MTV. Most definitely that was another example of what I did not want for my life.

Throw in a few sexually confusing elements such as witnessing your grandfather inappropriately kiss your classmate, be deceived by the majority of males that I encountered along with too many that didn't know how to respect boundaries and the man hater is born.

Hatred is nothing more than misplaced pain. There were still a few that conjured up the post caterpillars in my belly so I slipped and fell on occasion. Who doesn't like to blush? Unfortunately, I was much more vulnerable to rosy cheek tactics when I was feeling less than kosher which led me to accepting less than what I truly desired. Not quite getting the differences between lonely and alone, I wasted precious time with space fillers. Foolish mind games along the way always led to tears, recovery and reminders that men only wanted one thing and that black eyes were normal.

I decided that it was best not to allow anyone the opportunity to get close enough anymore to leave scars. Thus far I have gotten pretty skilled at this defensive play. Bad choices, failed attempts and elevated distrust when in the company of a man all led me to head-clearing celibacy. Men either saw it as a challenge or as no reason to stick around. I saw it as being a lose-lose situation and not worth the stakes. Throughout all of this, my basic needs were met by my own hands. I was the only person concerned if I had any good meals. No one else was going to care if I had socks for the winter, gas in the Ford, and bud in the pipe.

I maintained the bills on all that I needed and some that I wanted with my bi-weekly paycheck. I saw no reason to be tied to a man and had yet to meet one worthy of rope.

I stopped dating dogs and began rescuing them. It was trading one crutch for another but I had to wean off of the other somehow. Even more determined to live in my utopia where I did not have to allow anyone else to have any say, I did not allow anyone in at all. It just wasn't worth the tradeoffs anymore.

The pain for the fleeting moments lingered a little longer each time. I thought that time would heal all and I would be ready to try again when the right man was ready for me. I did not think that I would still be healing with seven and a half years under my belt. I found myself questioning why I was still taking out the trash and paying all of the bills out of my bank account alone. Even though I had learned the difference between lonely and alone, I found that lonely could be considered borderline suicidal. What I had not done was question why my mentality of survival mode had not changed in the least. So why did I expect it of my circumstances?

I had conditioned myself to survive without having to depend on anyone, much less a man. Straight, stubborn pride began growing barriers between my family and me. They had succeeded in making me feel so badly about myself that I was determined to make it on my own without ever having to ask them for help.

If per chance I did need to ask for something, I was vehement about repaying the favor before the kindness could be thrown back in my face during any given chastising moment. I kept everyone at a safe distance and the roller coasters flattened. But I like roller coasters. I find them exhilarating. Assuming I simply had not met the right man thus far, I buried myself in work. I lost myself in my causes. I did put a fair amount of effort into self-progression with eating less and moving around more. My job did and on occasion still does make me feel as if I just want to set the place ablaze.

Battling a physical ailment without even realizing it, the obstacles were abundant. My efforts should have paid off better and there were many moments of discouragement. I had definitely come a long way on my own when it came to my self-recovery, but I was starting to feel that I had made it as far as I was going to be able to solo.

The idea of opening up to the possibility of wanting, needing, and sharing with someone was a little scary and exciting at the same time. Welcome back, roller coaster. I remember the day I asked for help.

I was walking my dogs and feeling pulled in too many directions. Daisy Girl, my pit bull mix, was forging forward and dragging me like a rag doll. Enoch "Nucky" Thompson, my Chihuahua mix, was trying to engage me in a tug o' war with his leash behind me. I whispered a prayer for the New Year to include some guidance and support.

It was New Year's Eve and I was browsing Facebook with the little down time I had before getting ready to leave for an appointment. What? Wait. Go Back. "Free Chakra Readings. Donations accepted today and tomorrow."

With the telephone number, I found myself dialing as if it were natural. I knew I would have to do some crafty scheduling as my appointment was at the opposite end of the spectrum from her home. There was zero question in my mind that I would be there before the night was out.

What better way to start the New Year off with, by focusing on the next steps of my path?

Turns out my current path had me feeling dead on the inside. I found out I was functioning off of only one chakra, the Life chakra. I was assuming that it is kind of mandatory unless you plan on killing yourself.

I was only at the point of survival where the will to live did not seem to be enough. I had to find a way to do more than survive and maintain. The guidance that was shared with me on that night was invaluable; and that guidance was only the beginning of change.

My path was about to begin changing subtly and I would not have been drawn to her place had I not been ready to embrace what was next. Drop one not so good aspect of my life and replace it with a better habit. I had to do this at my own pace, as long as there was a pace. I made a list of anyone that I could think of that had hurt me in some manner. (People from my past, of course.)

It could have happened ten years ago, but if you got me to talking about it, my emotions would have you believing that it was just yesterday.

I left the dirty dishes in the sink to wash later so that I could get started on my first assignment after feeding my animals and myself. I had to write forgiveness letters that were to be burned on nights with full moons.

It was time for me to practice the art of letting go. From picking my battles better and holding my tongue more often as it is not for me to fix all that is wrong with the world.

I had to learn to let go of the last man that broke my heart in order to give the next one a fair chance. I also had to let go of other peoples' crap that I for some reason felt compelled to carry around.

I am making peace with some things from yesterday. What's done is done, so that I can make room for my tomorrow.

I also set up an altar in my home. I light a candle and just talk. I talk to my ancestors and ask for direction. I talk to my Higher Power about my fears, my laughter, my struggles and my dreams.

I have been surviving and maintaining for so long that I feel as if I am getting another chance to actually live. I will be armed with my tough lessons and a much better understanding of the necessity to set and enforce healthy boundaries. I will be better at knowing when it is time for them to cross, if at all.

147

I will not assume that every man is expecting something in return if I just shut up and allow him to buy me dinner. I will work on that letting a man be a man thing. I will make better choices and be okay with just me until my stars align with someone else's.

I will allow people more room to be themselves and accept that we all make mistakes. Give them more room to be human so that I can do the same for myself. Those indiscretions do not make up anyone as a whole. I will be more open to the unfamiliar. I will be willing to take more chances, especially if he is worth it.

I will find balance in helping others without deterring from the places inside of me that need my attention. I will stop allowing those that have hurt me yesterday to continue to do so tomorrow by holding on to unnecessary pain.

I have accepted that chances are I rarely, if ever, cross their minds and I am okay with that. Without compromising myself or my true aspirations, I will be more pliable.

My journey begins with searching for answers to things I have had trouble letting go of from my past to better understand my present so that I can be happy in my future. There is much to be learned from a creative child with a four pack of play dough.

Jessica Davis

Are You a Liability or an Asset?

One day I was talking to a girlfriend and she said he was calling it off. The wedding was off and there was no fixing it. Her fiancé had walked out. Every woman's question was: Was he justified, or was this an easy route out of what may have been forever? They had dated for several years but lived in separate households. There were no secrets but obviously some things were not addressed. These same non-secrets would ultimately be the demise of her relationship. In trying to plan their future, the fiancé did a financial assessment and found out more than he was willing to bear. She had a college loan she was paying for. She had some charge offs. Her credit score was in the low 500's. She had missed several payments on necessities (house note, car, etc.). She had a great job but did not bring home a lot because she had obligations to the IRS. She had baggage. She had undisclosed financial baggage. Maybe her telling him before he found out would have saved the day, maybe not. When he asked her what was all of "this," she could not explain. His response: "I can't afford to marry you" and he simply walked away. Ladies, assess your life, your lifestyle, and your debt. We are still foolishly trying to keep up with the Joneses when they cannot even keep up with themselves. Keep your monetary portfolio in perspective. Remember marriage is about love, but it is also about business and the sharing of information. Some people's love can overcome a student loan and a 30-day delinquency; some love cannot. Make sure that you bring as much to the table to never be obligated to another because you have less. There is nothing wrong with having less but know who you are having less with as well. Do your own due diligence. Wake up and make sure that he is not a liability as well; and, if he is, make sure your love and business can handle it. Think of marriage as a business fueled on money that needs the additive of love to balance out the solution. It's easy to love. It is not as easy to balance the checkbook of life. Think of Love as this: **Levelheaded decisions Outweigh Vanity Eternally (LOVE).**

Part III Healing

Healing Comes with Releasing

Pillar # 3

Self-Recovery

"Courage Consists in the Power of Self-Recovery"
Ralph Waldo Emerson

Admit...

No One Can Cure You but You

- I am powerless over my situation (whatever it is at the time) — that my life and quality of life have deteriorated and are now unmanageable.
- I believe that a Power greater than myself can renew me to the person God intends for me to be.
- I made a decision to turn my will and life over to the care of God. And, if I do not know Him, I will make a conscience effort to get to know Him so I can understand the changes and transitions He is about to place in my life.
- I will take a collective inventory of mind, body, soul, and spirit and ask God to renew me where I need to be renewed and heal me where I need to be healed.

- I will continue to take personal inventory and let God lead me to the treasures, rewards, and experiences in which He says I deserve more.

Self-recovery is a step in the healing process that involves digging deep and facing the hurt, pain, and future. Self-recovery means confronting your demons, conquering those demons and leaving those demons in the past. It does not involve retaliation. It does not involve revenge. It <u>does</u> involve letting go and being mature and woman enough for the man, woman, or situation that you're dealing with to let go and let God handle it. In this letting go and letting God, you also have the mental discipline to let go of the old you and look toward building the new you. It's like the transformation of a caterpillar to a butterfly. You will go through a transformation and leave behind old ways, but the new you will accomplish extraordinary feats and bless all who are around you. And the answer is yes! It is worth it.

Sad yet accepting guitar chords string their way into my head weaving a path for healing to begin.

One of those songs that refuses to be forgotten playing over and over and over again.

Resignation took over as I pressed repeat, silently settling down with my pen to write.

Shamelessly welcoming defeat, comforted by the cover of candlelight.

Already suffering from the engulfing heat, preparing for the burning demons I will soon fight.

Jessica Davis

Determined To Go To Bed Sober Tonight.

recovery [rɪˈkʌvərɪ]   n pl -eries

1. the act or process of recovering, especially from sickness, a shock, or a setback; recuperation

2. restoration to a former or better condition

3. the regaining of something lost

4. the extraction of useful substances from waste

Self-recovery is critical in one's mental and physical fortitude. We all have suffered from poor decision making. We have also suffered from some type of intentional or unintentional action of ourselves or another. The future of an individual is based on how she recovers from the ordeal. The first thing we must do is admit the truth and seek help if necessary.

One of the biggest problems that the female population faces is addressing mental health. Mental health is a subject that most are embarrassed to talk about or seek help for to overcome. In this fight for sanity and clarity, you must remember that it's you against the world and you must do whatever it takes to triumph over demons such as fear and embarrassment. Also, remember that when you take a step to help yourself, you make it easier for the next person having the same doubts to follow in your footsteps.

You must assess your situation and do what is best for you and your family. It may be a stressful task, but you are the queen who gives energy and light to a multitude of followers. Your family and friends look to you for strength, courage, and clarity. A society without a queen is a society lost.

He painfully sang of no sunshine for three long days.

I was relating per daytime work and nighttime inebriated ways.

Got me to thinking as my thoughts rolled over.

Could not do it in a tricky crossover.

Gave it a once over. Then a makeover. And still couldn't remember the last time I was sober.

It all came flooding how numb I had become. Emotions were next to none.

It was no longer fun. Steady on the run. Just ... Just ease my mind some.

I tried to remember ... I tried.

I tried to make it up and to myself I lied ... I tried.

And then I cried and I cried. Until it all began to collide and in myself I could once again confide.

Jessica Davis

New Kid on the Block

When I was a child, I always felt that I was often dealing with details that most other children were not: from molestation to domestic violence, mental illness and going to ten different schools by the time I was in the ninth grade.

I was not anywhere long enough to plant seeds or any true roots. I have pretty much been the "new kid" all my life. I was usually ashamed about whichever home situation I was dealing with and never felt that my peers would understand me, so there was never anyone for me to confide in.

Then there was CPS [Child Protective Services], and more moving, more picking up the pieces of my life and starting over. I became comforted by the tears on my pillow, for they were one of the only consistencies that I had.

Food was my first addiction being that it was the only thing that guaranteed me pleasure. As you can imagine, weight has been a struggle for me my entire life.

"How close was Jessica from becoming Miss America?," I remember the cruel seventh grader asking in front of everyone at the bus stop. "She only missed it by one foot. Six extra inches on each hip."

I smoked my first Marlboro Red in the fifth grade. Cigarettes did not become a habit until the tenth grade though and, by then, it was Marlboro Lights before becoming Newports.

Alcohol was pretty easy to get, as was weed. Some of my friends were moving on to powders, but I managed to avoid that one until Job Corps.

There was not much room left for me and addictions. Though money was an obstacle, cocaine and other drugs were unlimited when I attended there so it was easy to get.

After leaving Job Corps, I stopped using for a while, but picked it back up many years later with a co-worker. It was not long before the addiction spiraled out of control. And to make matters worse, my friend and I both got laid off from our jobs.

Once again, limited money hindered the growth of this particular addiction. Thank the Higher Powers above.

Though alcohol, weed and pills were front runners in my list of addictions, sex was not far behind.

I would stay awake if I had to face how I feel. So I'd instead pop a few pills.

Either through love or just a hormonal plan. Intoxicated was the only way I could lay down with a man.

Spent so much time convincing myself that I did not care. Hoping my feelings to spare.

Overcompensation causing not the best decisions to be made. From lines to bottles to where I laid.

I suppose there has always been a daddy complex of some sort; my father was not a constant figure in my life. I guess that is what made me very distrustful of men.

I watched my stepfather physically abuse my mother. I once witnessed a male family member kiss a classmate like he would have kissed a lover when I was a little girl.

Dealing with men has always been a fear of mine. More incidents than I care to admit where a man did not respect me, request limitations, and made me feel as if I did not count or matter and that only what I have between my legs was all that I had to offer. As you can imagine, I feel that men are very predatory which has made me defensive [over] time.

Relationships with women were not any better. I was molested by a teenage female family member before the age of ten. Even my feminine guidance and how to carry myself as a woman was limited due to my mother's paranoid schizophrenia.

The remaining female family members I had were prone to only point out the negative, all that I was doing wrong, while offering no alternative solutions.

[With the] lack of not having an example of any sort of healthy relationship and lacking appropriate boundaries, I began battling the feelings of being less than.

Being alone except for fleeting moments of unhealthy experiences did not help my growing self-image of self-hatred and unworthiness.

I would embark on short term, and less than what I wanted, needed or deserved type relationships. I was 'space filling' while waiting for the right one to come along, without recognizing that I was not being patient in my waiting.

I was passing the time as if minutes are not priceless and irreplaceable. I accepted less-than-I-deserved treatment just to have someone there.

They were as temporary as the numbing buzz I got from my drug of choice and left me feeling worse than the worst of hangovers. After, I would climb back into my shell for a long period of time to gather my thoughts and lick my wounds; I would shelter myself until I felt strong enough to try again.

Four hours of admissions and tears led to me embarking on a callous night of cold turkey.

Minus the Wild Turkey.

Not feeling strong enough to survive. Angry with myself for even thinkin' I'm good enough to try.

The severity of my need to not fail positioned me as a vulnerable flame in the wind.

Falling off of this horse even if only for the sleeping sun's time could very well be the end.

Of my tomorrows, leaving only wasted sorrows. No opportunities to try again.

Almost nonexistent hope and dwindling fight are depending on me for their survival as mine are leaning on them.

All circles are complete whether or not you make it all the way around while taking them for a spin.

Heartbreaking lesson I was forced to find. Life has no problem leaving you behind.

My heart rate becomes angrier the more the doubt tries to settle in.

My fists furiously tighten as the battle makes arrangements to begin.

The addiction to crutches creates panic attacks throughout my shocked veins.

They are not used to there being more blood than sedations and shame.

My liver is the only thing that doesn't miss the Comfort of the South or the tequila of the border.

I asked the higher powers to take some things from me and in no particular order. Just take them.

Steal nicotine cravings, burning Newports just to burn them. Not to inhale. Just burn them.

Thieve space filling with the company of a man that was never concerned with more than that.

I helped him take advantage of the low point I found myself in.

Becoming desperate enough, I looked in the mirror and became content with what I saw.

To cleanse my physical of toxins that hindered my sanitizing spiritually.

Things went on like this for years. I strapped myself into a hindering cycle of putting myself into positions that only hurt me further.

I was assuming that everyone eventually falls in love, eventually gets married, and eventually has kids.

I figured these events occurring in my life would put me on a better path. I knew it all would come in time. However, I finally had to acknowledge that no changes were going to come until I invited them in.

I was in my late twenties before I got angry enough and started doing something about it.

It started one night with one song on repeat for four hours. I had spent years knowing that a lot of 'some things' were wrong, but had no idea how to make them right, as well as having no idea what right would actually entail.

It is hard to set a goal that you cannot envision. That night was the first step, and I let go of all that I thought I knew. I cried like there was no feasible solution on the other side. I was finally accepting that it was myself that I needed to stop fighting with. United we stand and I was tired of crawling.

I did not have all of the answers, but I vowed to start climbing the steep incline of the obvious changes that I needed to make. Simply put, one foot in front of the other armed with only my gut talking to me and the knowledge that what I had been doing was not working.

It was time for exploration into alternative lifestyle changes. That particular year included the loss of my Mama, my job and two surgeries; the way I saw it, it was now or never.

About the same time that I began my self-recovery journey, I became a foster mom to a teenage boy who had accidentally killed someone.

There was no more time or room for self-pity and my victim thought patterns. It helps to follow a good game plan in your mind when you are leading someone else out of their dilemma.

To me, nothing speaks louder than leading by example. I had to think twice about every choice I made for he was watching. I did not want him drinking alcohol in excess, smoking cigarettes and popping pills so I acted accordingly.

It was not an overnight success, but I found moderation and walked a fine line and found a happy medium as best I could.

I had been diagnosed with depression and anxiety and his diagnosis was post-traumatic stress disorder. I found the doctors wanted us to lean on these medications that neither of us found to be beneficial at all. They were not preventing our symptoms and the impact to the pocketbook was not appealing at all.

When it came to the struggles of learning how to handle interactions with men, I maintained. I made a decision to abstain from sex. It was not easy to do at all. We all want to feel wanted and desired. I think the intimacy was the aspect I missed the most.

I did not want to waste time and energy on space fillers and rebounds. I was also setting an example for my 'son' by showing him how to treat a lady.

He was very protective of me so I did not want any tension in the home that I was not ready to defend. He had to be a special dude to be introduced at home. Along the way, I got to know myself and what I found to be pleasurable without the clutter of temporary.

Pleading to know that alone is beautiful and that lonely can be survived.

Knowing the difference between the two is vital to be able to thrive.

Learning to love myself along the way while wanting to remember what happened last   night.

It could very well be just one evening.   It may be just everything's beginning.

Ready to give my all to take on this bout.   It is imperative that I find out.

I still don't know all that is right.   And this is only the beginning of my fight.

As I hold myself tight. Turn out the lights. Determined To Go To Bed Sober Tonight.

One of the most valuable lessons that I learned throughout all of this was the difference between lonely and alone. Being alone can be fabulous. Lonely can be suicidal. I learned how to better manage the two once I actually gave merit that they had a true difference.

I did some spring cleaning to my existence and gave more notice to quality as opposed to quantity.

I will always be a work in progress, seeking quality, for I have become smarter about wasting time with people and things that I will only have to kick out of my life later.

I began to pay more attention to what I truly wanted and made plans to acquire it. I began implementing patience and actually holding out for what I wanted instead of just taking whatever was within my reach.

I began addressing all of my addictions and finding healthier options to replace them with. When there was nothing else, I taught myself to accept that the only preference was to wait until the real thing came along.

I stopped spending so much time in drive thrus. Most of that "food" was not actually food at all. It became clear that I would be paying for cheap convenience no matter what. I surmised that a meal worth eating is a meal worth proper preparation.

I became aware that I needed to eat for nourishment and not for pleasure. I cut out things that I never thought I could live without, like sodas.

I used to hear "You should drink more water." To which I replied, "There is water in my soda," without realizing how ignorant I really sounded. Health and hygiene mattered to me much more in a transparent manner.

I began searching for ways to get healthy and flavorful to coincide. I began to gravitate towards organic goods. I began avoiding foods with colors, hormone injections and preservatives.

If a Twinkie lasts for seven years on your pantry shelf, imagine how long it takes your body to break it down. Many ingredients that our bodies do not recognize and do not know what to do with just hangs around for a while setting up shop in your thighs.

I did things like substituting a small plate of raw veggies and dressing for a greasy side of fries or chips. I also came to the understanding that diet alone was not going to get me closer to my preferred dress size. It was not going to be adequate on its own to make me feel more vigorous.

I commenced to explore the world of exercise and fitness from DVDs to classes. I started with belly dancing, walking with my dogs, yoga and hula hoop dancing.

It is good to have a variety to battle the excuses of the elements and outside influences. My belly dancing was on DVD if I needed to do something inside. My dogs are always game for a walk with me. Yoga is wonderful for stretching, flexibility and body maintenance.

Every so often I will get on my bicycle and even turned my walk into a tiny jog. I fell in love with the feminine beauty, sexy hip strokes and creative outlets that hula hoop dancing provides.

I put on my Ipod and danced like no one was watching, even though someone usually does stop to stare for a moment, which gave me an added incentive to keep the hoop up.

Motivation can be fleeting, so I found things that I enjoyed and I used them to keep me going.

Physical exercise affects mental health. I came to understand my mental state needed a serious work out too. For me, writing was a way that I could stimulate my brain.

I participated in open mics. I joined a Write Club to surround myself with other writers and get some inspiration.

In addition, reading was another way that I like to exercise my mind.

I also got involved with some causes that I deemed to be important to me. I put a whole lotta' heart into animal rescue. I volunteered to fight for the right to legalize marijuana. I pursued projects that would contribute to the direction of my dreams. Basically, I found what mattered to me and focused on those things.

One day I realized that there was nothing left to devote to the things that were derogatory to my well-being. That included wasting time with the wrong man.

I still hope to find the one to grow old with and commit myself to, but he has to fit into the world that I have created for myself.

I will not be bending or compromising myself anymore as I have in the past to make something work that was never meant to be.

If it is right, our worlds will mesh together with not so many hurdles.

I have also gotten much more successful at facing my 'less than' perfect mindset I had for so long. I will no longer lean on crutches and splints; there will be no more stitches, staples or masking tape for me. Of course, I still encounter obstacles intended to deter me from my path and regress my well-earned progress, but I am quicker to recognize them for what they actually are.

My journey to self-recovery has also given me a well-defined and pristine view of the absolutely gorgeous lady smiling back at me from the mirror and she is not so bad. I am very glad that I rediscovered who she was and we get along very well, the way best friends should.

Jessica Davis

When you give up on yourself, you give up on family. You diminish the family unit when you are not at your best. It is a difficult challenge, nevertheless a challenge that must be overcome. We cannot be effective family units without the resilience and strength of mothers, sisters, grandmas, and aunts. Without this, we are like veins without blood.

Pillar # 4

Forgiveness

"Getting to Know Yourself, Letting Go of the Past, and Embracing the Future"
Rickie Chaffold

Relax...Relate...Release
Don't let un-forgiveness kill you.

- Forgiving releases the shackles that deny and stagnate growth.
- Realizing and addressing present, past, and future thinking patterns affect your ability to forgive.
- Do not be ashamed of the mistakes ... be proud of the decision to correct them.
- Do not let denial or the act of forgiving yourself or others hold you hostage.
- The road to infinite possibilities does not begin until you say, "I forgive myself and I forgive YOU."

Realize that you also hurt yourself when choose not to forgive. If you do not realize anything, realize and embrace this point. Non-forgiveness leads to stress, high blood pressure, ulcers, headaches, and many other mental and physical health issues. The question: Why give a person or situation that you don't care for so much power over your mental and physical health and happiness? Your epiphany is that you have the power to forgive and it will benefit you, the trespasser, and your loved ones in the future.

Realize that there is a balance in forgiving. Forgiveness does not contradict responsibility of behavior. Forgiveness is a present that you give to yourself. It is emancipation from the affliction of anger and pain. Choosing to forgive allows you to have power over your choices and enhances the decision making process. Making decisions with an unforgiving heart can make the decision making process cloudy. It can affect decisions that have nothing to do with the unforgiving situation. Forgiving allows us to live in the present and the future instead of the past. Forgiving should be a process of learning. Some people say, "Don't forget." We say, "Forget" because you have learned from that mistake and will be alert to the signs of the same if it crosses you again. And if it does, the next time you will deal with the situation accordingly. Learning from forgiving is a release to move forward with the one you love. When you forgive and release yourself, you also release the loved ones around you from being subjected to living with a person with an unforgiving heart. Forgiveness doesn't happen on its own; you must choose to forgive.

Forgiveness

The beauty of forgiveness is not only releasing someone else from the negative energy associated with them. You are also freeing yourself.

I Forgive ... Do You?

She looks in the mirror wondering, "How did I get to this place?" She does not even recognize herself anymore. Her world is in shambles. Embarrassingly, she has not talked to God in quite some time and feels at a loss regarding reaching out to Him now.

She has gained weight due to the stress of the situation, she cannot concentrate at work because thoughts of "him" keep distracting her, and slowly but surely she has managed to push away almost everyone she loves because she was tired of them "getting in her business."

Now, she is exactly where she said she wanted to be: alone.

When entering into relationships, most women are taught to be strong, independent, supportive, smart and nurturing. However, often when they think "this is love," they forget the importance of the wisdom suggested to them.

In that instance, God and the new partner's positions switch. He becomes her sole focus; she is devoted and dedicated to him with all of her energy. Yet when it all goes bad, there stands a woman scorned! Angry at him, herself and the world, she is feeling resentful and bitter because she cannot bring herself to forgive him and just let it go.

She is walking around holding all of the hurt of being in a relationship with a human being while losing her connection with God, even if it is momentarily.

"It wasn't supposed to end like this." "She was supposed to be getting married." "He said he loved me!!! He said he would be here forever and that I would not have to search anymore because, at last, my love had come along." "How could he lie like that? How could he have done that to me and I gave him everything?!?" " I did everything for him ..."

Now she sits in silence, re-evaluating everything. What was he accountable for? What part did she have to play? Where did his responsibility end and hers begin? She starts to realize something: "I put him before God."

With time comes clarity, and with clarity comes resolve. Once you get past your emotions, you come to logic and understanding. She now understands that "all men are not alike." "Every man is not out to hurt me. I will survive this and will love again. Only next time I will do it differently. The type of man that I end up with is who I choose to be with; it's my responsibility to choose well."

In the silence, she starts to desire to reconnect with God. Through prayer she is able to start to release the pain, resentment and blurred perceptions that she's developed about *men and relationships and it gives her a sense of freedom. As she reconnects to God and starts to release the emotion she has been holding onto, her life starts to normalize.*

A peace starts to develop in her spirit and she is starting to get back to her old self. She even got her loved ones back. They joined her in prayer circles.

There is life after hurt and mistakes and she will be okay. It may take a while for her to completely get over it, but she knows that in time she will forgive herself and eventually forgive him, too.

"I release all disappointment from my mental, physical, spiritual and emotional body. 'Cause I know that Spirit guides me and love lives inside me. That's why today I take life as it comes."
– Healing by India Irie

Sacha Simmons

I Wish You Well

I never envisioned the day that I would be without the love of my life. Although we had a bittersweet relationship, I thought that when the end of the day came, he would be mine and of course I was his. Without a second guess, he had power that made the hairs stand at attention when he entered any room. I secretly had a love for my husband that I strongly felt would stand the test of time.

With three children all two years apart, a new mortgage and plans for a successful life, things were finally turning around after all the drama we had been through since we had met.

We were nineteen and seventeen when we married, and we were very committed. Sometimes I think, wow, had we signed a contract for destruction?

I would give this man whatever he wanted only to get partial love in return, but I stayed and prayed because I knew that the day would come that he would get better and finally understand the concept of God first, family second, work, then friends and fun.

So many days I felt all alone trying to work, raise our three children, finish school, cook and clean with no help. I knew the day of change would come.

Inevitable visions are the worst. I would manage to find strength to give him his 'medicine' daily before he left for work because I would not dare give him room to say that I did not make love to him as much as he needed it. Also, I made it a point that he would always have a home-cooked hot meal prepared before he left for work at night because that was my man ... my equal ... my mate.

The more and more I did to accommodate our relationship, the further and further I felt him drift away. I knew the day would come, but I forgave him and I forgave myself for staying.

Holidays, birthdays, or even just because ... his investment, nothing ... my investment, forgiving. The children ... his investment, nothing. No happiness to see them. No "daddy loves you" ... no surprises for them, nothing ... my investment for them, forgiving and praying.

The day came in 2006 when I woke up from what seemed to be a nightmare to only realize I was not dreaming. All that I had hoped and dreamed for was soon about to come to an end.

Why?

There was another besides me and my children. Another that had no ... (maybe she did) inclination to the fight ... struggle ... burden it was keeping my husband, children, and household together.

I found out that she did know, but she simply did not care. I forgave and I prayed. I thought about hurting her ... and giving her a piece of what I had given all the others before her.

Yes, before her, there were many others. I stayed, I prayed, I forgave. But this time, that day was finally here and I gave him exactly what he was looking for, his freedom from his three children and [me].

My marriage ended with no plans, no structure, no support and no direction. My decision was hasty, but I had to remove myself and our children from this very hurtful and now dangerous equation.

All respect and boundaries were broken. I was extremely angry, hurt, bitter ... but I prayed. No one cared about my feelings ... I know he did not nor did he know how to.

I recall a conversation on my living room sofa with him ... I asked him to stop ... but to no avail. Too little, too late and the non-empathetic way he handled this is buried in my soul to this day ... but I pray.

Bitter and angry, I have tried to pick up the pieces and move on with my three children. I try to limit conversations and accidental encounters with the both of you. But for some reason, "leaving well enough alone" with him has turned my life into a living hell.

I thought, "Who are you?" I continued to pray and tried to stabilize my life as much as possible, but the memories, divorce, and the broken picture keeps chasing me.

It is only because of the Blood of the Lamb that I am still sane, and you are still here. I continue to pray. I spend days and nights crying and depressed because I did not sign up for any of this.

I look back and it seems blurry now, but I am so glad I am starting to come through this. One day when I thought it was all crashing down on me, I had an epiphany. Something hit me like electricity going through water.

I gave him power. I allowed him to manifest my destiny by simply not forgiving him. I prayed but I still held on to the resentment, anger, and the hate I had for him and his actions.

It is still trial and error at this point, but I can stand strong and say that part of my life is over.

He will no longer be able to take my happiness, peace and joy. I have simply decided to close the door on that portion of my life, by leaving it in the past.

I closed the door by wishing him the best in his endeavors with him. It is natural to say that God is good. I believe in Karma. I hope you do as well.

I would not wish on anyone (well, maybe him from time to time) the pain that I went through. Yes, I know better now, and I am doing better!

I also closed the door on having sex with him and leaving trails of evidence to show his fiancé that he is not in love with her as he claimed to love his three children and [me].

Today, I choose to open the door to forgiveness and allow the peace and happiness that I know I deserve to manifest in my life. I am worthy of everything that was taken from me overnight.

I open the door to speak restoration over my soul. You did not give it to me. I promise I will no longer allow you to take it away. I will walk with my head held high from now on. I will be equally yoked again through forgiveness.

You said GOD sent my husband to you. If you believe that, I will believe it with you and I will wait for who God really has in store for me.

I wish you both peace and blessings in all that you do.

Rhodesia

Why Should I Forgive?

Anyone that knows me will tell you that I could hold onto a grudge like a dog holds onto his favorite bone. Forgiveness was never my strong point. I could forget what caused the rift in a relationship, but still refuse to part my lips and speak. I knew that they at one time committed some act of betrayal against me, so I refused to let go of the anger and hurt. I used silence as a weapon against the people that hurt my pride and my heart. It didn't matter how long ago that it happened; I refuse to let go. It took a long time for me to realize I was hurting myself more in the long run by holding onto these grudges. I always felt anxious and tense; I could never seem to relax. I had more than my share of restless nights. It wasn't until an intense conversation with my mother that I realized what the true problem was.

Holding onto grudges crowds your heart and mind with negative feelings. Those negative feelings cause you to feel anxious, depressed, and angry. If you are consumed with negativity, it makes it impossible for you to enjoy anything positive. Refusing to forgive someone allows them to have control over your emotions and your life. The resentment and bitterness that you feel carries over to new relationships. Forgiving someone can be a very painful and difficult process, but it's necessary. Forgiveness doesn't mean that you deny the other person's responsibility for hurting you, and it doesn't minimize or justify the wrong. You can forgive the person without excusing the act. As you let go of grudges, you'll no longer define your life by how you've been hurt. By forgiving someone, it allows you to feel peace. Once I decided to make a real commitment to do this, a lot of things changed for me. I felt less anxiety and stress and developed stronger relationships. I began enjoying the small things in life. Forgiveness brings a kind of peace that helps you go on.

How can anyone be completely happy when they are loaded down with resentment and bitterness? How can you expect God to forgive you if you can't forgive others? You limit your blessings when you hold onto past hurt and anger. Usually people that can't forgive others also have a harder time forgiving themselves. Forgiving yourself or another isn't easy, but it is the gateway to freedom. The value of forgiveness is priceless.

Contrina Jenkins

~Forgiveness is a blessing that affords you peace and favor (no plans, no structure, no support and no direction) when you lose your way in the midst of a storm.~

Healing begins with forgiving yourself and others and loving yourself. Healing is not about loving someone who hurt you mentally or physically. Your duty to yourself was simply to forgive them so you could move on with your best days. To love one's self is the beginning of a lifelong romance; I promise, you should try it if you have not already! Falling in love with yourself will allow growth and clarity never seen and never told. Healing one's self – mind, body, soul – allows forgiveness of self and others for transgressions and wrong decisions committed against you.

There are two sides of healing.

You have to heal from things you do to yourself and from things that others do to you. Things that we do to ourselves start with decisions made rationally and irrationally. Most irrational decisions are based on emotions. Whether it was that gut feeling, anger, or sympathy, it was a decision based on emotion. We must get out of this train of thought if we are going to be successful. We must STOP making emotional decisions. We must train ourselves to not only rely on intuition, but also to rely on the facts and circumstances that influence the decisions that will be made. At the end of the day, your decision should be positive, make sense for the present and future, and allow you to be at peace with your decision ... no regrets.

We must start training our mentalities to act and react in a positive way. This simple practice will allow us to make better decisions. This practice will also allow forgiveness of self freely with no regrets.

Unfortunately, it is easier to forgive ourselves than it is to forgive others. The hurt and pain can be unbearable but there is a way, a will, and a destiny for you to forgive whoever has betrayed and taken advantage of you. The sooner you forgive, the sooner you can heal. The sooner you heal the easier it will be to make rational decisions. Not forgiving is the force that will have overwhelming influence and detrimental impacts on our decision making.

Forgiving Yourself

We often do not forgive ourselves and this manifests in the reflection that we see when we look in the mirror. Manifestation of negative self-esteem, beauty, and one's worth are the result of guilt and un-forgiveness.

Self-Esteem

You are the only one that counts. Today is the last day that what someone says about you will affect you ... no matter if it is truth or false. Self-esteem means that your positive outlook of self trumps whatever anyone's opinion is of you.

One of the leading causes of poor and bad decision making is a direct result of having poor self-esteem. Having a lack of self-esteem seemingly sends out some type of signal to those who love to take advantage of the innocent and trusting.

Poor self-esteem stems from many things. Your character, weight, socioeconomic and popularity status, and your sexual preference all can uplift or tear down your self-esteem.

The key to overcoming low self-esteem is to know that you are strong, beautiful, and a force to be reckoned with.

You must believe in yourself so that other people will have no other choice but to believe in you. You must set a precedent for your existence and success.

Two key factors in your success are empowerment and perception. Love whom you see in the mirror, no matter the reflection. Always remember that you are under divine protection. Your beauty lies within your strength to have faith.

Beauty

The things and people we see and interact with, the way we look at ourselves, and the way we want to be seen influence our daily decisions about beauty.

The interesting and saddening thing is the way the craziness in this society has us judging, not loving, and acting in a self-conscious manner about our internal and external beauty.

The beauty of self should be like self-esteem, but too often we are asking for permission from society to love and appreciate ourselves. How dysfunctional is that?

Well, ladies, it stops today.

Self-esteem is about self and no one else! Loving yourself starts with you! No one else. We are going to put society on the back burner. Short, tall, wide, or small, we dare you to look in the mirror, love yourself, and tell yourself that you are beautiful!!

These are things we all have heard, like beauty is only skin deep. Is that true? In some cases, it is and most cases it is not. I know some very attractive people on the outside that are the ugliest and most bitter people on the inside.

I also know some beautiful people who let society cripple them. Have you tried to understand these people? Are you one of them? We ask because deep inside everyone wants to be accepted but the main thing people miss out on is self-acceptance.

Beautiful people, stand up and be recognized. Just remember that your beauty starts with YOU defining it, you and no one else.

You have been in control before, now it is time to exercise the positive assertion of that control.

I am beautiful, it starts now and it starts with me!

"She Was So Beautiful"

She had the body of a goddess, her make-up was flawless She had roller coaster curves that made men nauseous And women would grab their men and become overcautious Just in case her perfect face decided to make their relationships a target Because she was so beautiful Women would degrade her downplay her say her beauty was false With comments like "I bet she doesn't look that good if she takes all that make-up off "She had charisma, she had confidence and women would assume That she was conceited and thought she was all of that because she could have any man in the room because she was so beautiful And I couldn't understand why they were paying her so much negative attention Tearing her down with their insecurities and opinions And the more they talked the more I listened But not one time did I hear that sister mention that she was so beautiful They said it for she didn't in this story she's the victim Because women don't see a sister they see competition They see skin and hair, they see clothes and shoes They don't realize she goes through the same things they do She has to deal with disrespect being treated like a sex object Sexual harassment at the workplace just to get a check because she is so beautiful Just like them, but sisters can't get past their jealousy, envy and pride So they judge her before getting to know who she is inside You see being pretty can be pretty painful and it's sad that being beautiful has to hurt And it's sad that we judge an outer appearance instead of getting to know her first So she takes glamour shots but not those in a photo shoot or photo booth But those low blows like "she's a prostitute" or "those ain't her real eyes" "that ain't her real hair" "she know she's wrong for that outfit she could have found something else to wear" "she's got stretch marks, she must have kids" "she ain't got no breasts" "girl her breasts are too big" "she's too skinny" "she's too fat" "she's too this and she's too that" "she thinks she's the cute one in the bunch look at her friends" She is so beautiful she just can't win Beautiful beauty but there is a beast within and her sisters beat her down for being beautiful so now she tries to pretend like she is ugly And her outer beauty creates a monster inside that does ugly things Gives her more insecurity and lowers her self-esteem Or she might become vain and promiscuous, and after becoming burnt out on broken relationships and giving her best to men She might find safety and security in her same sex and become a lesbian Because another woman is affectionately telling her that she is so beautiful So many women are uncomfortable with themselves so they hate and say stuff They need to take a look in the mirror and take off the make-up And I'm not talking about fashion fair, Mary Kay or Mac I'm talking about your emotional make-up and the baggage that's attached Before you say something negative about a sister consider how you sound At that point you are a crab in the bucket Why do you want to pull her down? And then some sisters will say "I'm just speaking my mind" Well I think your thoughts are clouded and your big mouth is blocking her shine Because you can't find substance in your face, you can't find substance in your shape It has nothing to do with how thin or thick you are, it has nothing to do with your weight And you can't find substance in your status, clothes, car or your job The only place you can find long lasting substance is in GOD So if you've been crying out through your actions, if you've been crying real tears Wipe your face dry your eyes and let those negative comments fall on deaf ears Because when GOD made you he made you beautiful And he knew he made a gem So if any of you have something negative to say direct your comments to Him And she will still be beautiful

Se7en

Relationships and Real Estate

While consoling a friend one day who had just suffered a breakup, I was blessed to deliver a modern parable. My friend is beautiful, successful, and talented and knows how to treat a man; yet, she was dumped for a woman who did not share the same attributes and who lacked class and style.

She was devastated and baffled by this and began to measure herself to the other woman. She even began to doubt who she was. Dismayed by this, I challenged her to examine the man. He was not necessarily a bad guy, just unhappy with his life. He had been on the same job that he hated for over 16 years, was constantly struggling and felt that he was not hip or cool.

My friend on the other hand is a bonified celebrity who travels the world and is effortlessly hip. Hmmm ... wonder why he jumped ship? Well, this is the story I told her and I hope it blesses and inspires you as well.

I told her to envision herself as a million dollar home that had been on the market for some time with no buyers. After some time, she decides to lease herself out to a man who is unqualified to purchase that value of the home, just to have someone occupy the empty space.

While in the home, the man realizes the maintenance and upkeep involved with that type of space. He loves the home but is unable to furnish it properly, keep the grounds or even pay the high utility costs! He doesn't really fit in with the neighbors who can afford the lifestyle associated with that type of home. Nor does he have a plan to elevate himself to fill the space. He decides that he would be happier in a simpler home where he can feel like a king in his palace, not a pauper in hers. So he breaks the lease and finds a home better suited to his needs and standards.

Now the house stands empty again, with some visible wear and tear from the last tenant. Although it was not abused, it hadn't been properly maintained. The floors needed cleaning, a fresh coat of paint, the garden groomed. Nothing major and it could go back on the market! Only one problem: This is not a seller's market. As one looked around the neighborhood, you could see its decline. Other homes in the community had been through similar experiences. Homes were being bought but for significantly less than what they were worth. Some homes had been foreclosed on (broken marriages). Some remained empty or abandoned. Very few were filled with happy families.

So what do you do to maintain your value when your neighborhood has declined? You have to come together and form an association whose common goal is to raise the market value of their community. One of the first duties of the association is to establish the community by putting a gate around it (body of Christ). This ensures that not just anyone can come into the community, unless God our gatekeeper lets them enter. The next duty is to evict tenants who are abusing and neglecting the properties in the community (serve them their notice through prayer and watch God move them out). Next is clean up time. Some homes are in need of repair and remodeling, and this requires more than just faith but also action! After that, it's time to get beautified. When the foundation is solid and the house has been cleaned, furnishings, art, décor, flowers and fragrance complete a home for showing.

Now back to the buyers.

While some men are content leasing their space in life, a good man wants to own his. Beware of the man that only wants the lease out of life. Is it that he feels he is incapable of buying (he knows his credit score, not yours)? Is it that he wants to occupy every home on the block? If so, how will he properly maintain them all? Either way, you lose.

Keep leasing and you will surely become rundown over time with no equity to show at the end of the day. Hold out for the right buyer, while improving your home. If you feel your home is complete, go and help another woman in your association complete hers. Remember: her value affects yours.

As for the buyers with so many homes off the market and under construction, they are limited and will be forced to either dwell in the projects or become qualified. Do you really want a man who would rather dwell in the dumps rather than work to qualify?

Bridgett Washington

You are not going to like what you see every time you look in the mirror. You must recognize what you do not like and establish what the negotiables and non-negotiables are for yourself. That's right: you must have standards and you must be flexible at the same time. You must have non-negotiables for yourself before you put non-negotiables into the atmosphere. Why would anyone listen to your list until you have been true to yourself with your own respect and definition of what your worth is to the world?

Pillar # 5

Self-Renewal

"The soul is placed in the body like a rough diamond and must be polished, or the luster of it will never appear.

~Daniel Defoe

Ask yourself these questions:

- What is my purpose?
- Am I happy with my life and what do I need to do to improve it?
- Do I have plan ... family plan, a professional plan ... a me plan?
- Are my spirit, mind, and body healthy?

Realize that, unless you take some time to care for yourself, you will be in no position to function properly for yourself or for the ones you love. Your professional and personal life demands prioritization, concentration, frugalness, empathy, fairness, and consistency. To balance all of this, one must make sure that they always recharge the inner being/nucleus so that it can process and produce positive results outwardly through actions and words. Daily renewal is vital for you to manage your mind, body, soul and spirit to be at your best when faced with the challenges of life. Rebuild, rejoice, and refocus. With the stress of daily life, renewal is necessary for survival. Healthy mental processing comes with clarity. Clarity is afforded by pressing the rest and reset buttons. The most organized and productive person needs a break. The path to renewal like everything else comes with a plan. You must schedule a reset – whether they are small breaks throughout the day or mini vacations in meditation, yoga, physical and mental exercise or whatever you find relaxing. Be honest in your renewal. Renewal is a part of the healing process. Renewal is a part of the forgiving process. Renewal is the only pillar that is a part of the other 8 pillars. You will constantly renew yourself while navigating the other 8 pillars. Renewal will keep you fresh and open minded to take on whatever crosses your path. Renewal will engage patience, humility, transparency, and new criteria with self-awareness. Renewal allows you to realize that you are you and your purpose is ordained by God. You have a mission and a vision that must be fulfilled.

Self-renewal is just that: It starts with you. It is so simple that people make the thought process complex when it comes to this pillar. Self, me, I and no one else have the power to change. See, we all have the power to change but we make excuses … the children, job, weight, age … STOP the madness. If you want change, you have the power to change you by answering one question: Do you want a better life? The answer is yes and it starts with you. We have figured out that you make everyone better around you; so the better you are, the better they (collectively) will be. You must realize that this is a factor that works with adverse consequences. When you are at your worse, they will be at their worse (collective) – a lot of pressure but it's true. Who can kiss a boo-boo and stop the tear? Who can lift him up from being torn down and remind him it's okay? Who can tell her best friend that it will be okay and she finds the energy and strength to hang in there (glass ceiling, cheating husband, children on drugs)? Renewal of you is not asking to be superwoman but instead realizing your value and worth to the dynamics that you influence just by being you or the best you that you can be.

Mentality

Ironically a woman's worth starts with how she feels about herself. Self-esteem is exactly that, self-esteem. Ladies you have to praise yourself and give yourself a compliment if no one else is giving them to you. Beauty starts from within. You must realize that there will be good days and bad days and that you have to have a plan for bad days. You must put yourself on a pedestal before someone else does.

Let's not get it twisted. This does not mean that you are better. This means be self-fulfilled and sufficient. Love yourself before someone else loves you (you don't love or understand yourself but expect someone else to love you [ridiculous]). Buy yourself flowers, take yourself to the movies and dinner, embrace your positives and your negatives, and have a plan to do better in both.

Beauty starts from smiling at yourself in the mirror and accepting you, to hugging yourself every day and expressing to yourself the appreciation that you have for you.

20/20 Vision = Maturity

For years, choosing who I wanted in my life, going where I wanted to go, living where I wanted to live, and buying what I wanted to buy required me to truly have it all together.

Reassess your life and understand wholeheartedly that what you have does not define who you are, but potentially puts you in the worst place possible.

It makes you the person that you dread being ... unhappy and in debt! Why do we believe that we must have certain things and look the part to fit in?

As children we are taught not to succumb to peer pressure and be a leader and not a follower, but that is truly the person we turn out to be as adults. We turn into the world's biggest flunky!

Following the belief that things determine your status creates a false sense of validation. As a woman, your security and motivation must come from within. When it does not, we become bogged down with what we think we are supposed to do. When our fathers do not give us a sense of security, we look to men and things.

"Daddy, when are you coming to get me?" That was my question every Thursday night – hoping, wishing, and praying that he would oblige. Well, he never did, and I grew up looking for a man to take care of me and make sure I was picked up on Friday and that a gift would follow.

Now, it never mattered to me if I had to spend an arm and a leg to impress that first time, because after that he would be mine. Now that I am experienced, I know none of it was free and I was trying to prove myself to someone who did not even know who they were.

When you try to fill voids, you will always find yourself trying to keep up with the Joneses. You ask who they are. They are the people who make it all look easy. The life, money, friends, purses, family, and toys that everyone sees not knowing what it took for them to acquire what we think is the "LIFE."

From the outside looking in, it looks wonderful but you would never know that they wish they had the life you did, and that they had people who really loved them. They also wish that their lives were simple.

When you seek God and find out who you are and what your purpose is, what used to matter goes out of the window. God states in Jeremiah 29:11 that He has a plan for our lives from before we were created in our mother's womb.

The plan is for us to acquire wealth, be in good health, and that our souls prosper. You cannot do this when your eyes are on people and not your purpose.

A woman's worth is far above what she can imagine according to Proverbs 31. If you do not seek out your purpose and destiny, you will never understand the plan for your life.

I was that chick that grew up with the best of everything. When I became an adult, I bought and had the best of everything and was exposed to the finer things of life.

Now that I am a mature adult, I understand that it is not what I have but who I am that counts.

Carla Stewart

Health

Too many of us are dying because of ignorance. Ignorance is no longer an excuse because you should know better. When you know better, you have to do better. Failure is not an option. How can you make a difference if you are not here? AIDS, high blood pressure, cancer, and domestic violence are killing women by the dozens every day.

Maintenance of the Mind

The mind is a very complicated and very important part of the human body. Once the mind is gone, all else will fail to perform properly.

Maintenance of the mind is extremely important if we want to lead a healthy life. The mind is affected by so many factors and is constantly being challenged daily.

In order to keep it sharp, we have to learn how to think properly. Thoughts can either make or break you. Even though it may not seem like it, we control our thoughts. We control what we think and how we react to what we think about.

We can think ourselves into so many different emotions and some can even cause bodily harm. What we think can make us feel joy or pain, angry or happiness, sickness or wellness. We have the control to think our way through a healthy or a miserable life.

You can think your way into illness, unhappiness, bad moods, misery, cheerfulness, joy or pain. You control these thoughts.

Your mind is a playground for the enemy. He deceives you and once you have been deceived in your thoughts, he can take over your body, your life, and you will begin to only exist and not live.

The enemy tells you lies. Your mind will begin to believe it and you will begin to live it. Keeping a sharp mind and maintaining it is truly necessary. I remember hearing my grandmother say, "An idle mind is the devil's playground."

A crisis is defined as something that you have no control over. You did not cause it nor can you control it. Often, you cannot control circumstances.

We often feel like we have no outlet. Your mind goes into a whirlwind and you face the possibilities of losing all that you thought to be normal.

Our everyday lives can take a toll on our mental state. Sometimes we do not respond to a crisis very well and it often can destroy us. So many times our minds shut down when faced with a crisis or change and, simply because we have not learned to think our way through situations, panic sets in.

Nothing works well in chaos. Therefore, we must keep a sharp and open mind. When dealing with crisis, we cannot just stand by idly and do nothing.

We must do something. If the mind is not sharp and filled with healthy thoughts, it will not be able to handle challenges in a healthy manner and we will shut down.

The mind is very fragile and can be affected without us even realizing how much it has impacted our mental capacity.

For most women, having a sound mind can seem sometimes unobtainable. Women face so many difficulties in life that it is important to keep your mind sharp and clear of infectious thoughts that can cause you to destroy yourself.

Self-destruction is the leading cause of a lot of the problems we face today. Often, we are the reason things are happening in our lives and spiral into difficult situations.

Allowing unhealthy thoughts to take over and keep you from living a purposeful life is not what God intended.

Romans 12:2 states, "Do not conform to the patterns of this world, but be transformed by the renewing of your mind. Then you will be able to test and approve what God's will is — His good, pleasing and perfect will."

The renewal of your mind is a must in order to change your life. Your thoughts are a direct connection to the quality of life you live. Proverbs 23:7 reminds us, "For he is the kind of person who is always thinking about the cost. 'Eat and drink,' he says to you, but his heart is not with you."

If you think something long enough, it will become reality. Hence, as a person speaks, so he is. You convince yourself to do or not to do something. The maintenance of your mind must be done. We have to renew our minds on a regular basis.

Ephesians 4:23-24 tells us (verse 23): "to be made new in the attitude of your minds; (verse 24) "and to put on the new self, created to be like God in true righteousness and holiness."

You have to change your thinking in order to be whole. The enemy will take over your mind and filter it with negativity to discourage you to do things. To have narrow thinking is to have a very narrow life. You have to do it; no one else can do it for you.

We are in control of our thoughts. I did not believe this at first. But, I began to combat negative thoughts with positive ones. You can wake up and start your day off thinking of all the negative things that happened to you the day before or choose to think only positive thoughts.

The enemy has an agenda for you the moment you open your eyes. He fills your mind with leftover negativity that you did not deal with the day before.

So, what do we do? We revisit those thoughts and begin to think of ways to deal with them. The toughest enemy you will ever face is you.

Have you ever realized that thoughts and emotions are the only things that cannot be dealt with physically? Let me be clear: We take out our thoughts and emotions physically and verbally on others every day. But when was the last time you slapped a thought, beat down an emotion, choked a fear ... do you get it now?

We cannot beat down negative thoughts and emotions by pounding them out of our heads or taking them out on others whether they deserve it or not.

So what do we do? Usually when something attacks us negatively, we are able to lash out or retaliate physically and verbally. But now that you know better, it is time to act better. Act and react are the key words here. You have to process other actions and react to those actions differently (New You). We have to think and act differently. Why? Because we have redefined our purpose and our purpose is to always be the best we can be (New You). No one's actions should dictate yours. You must have your own agenda for success and your agenda may be the answer to whomever or whatever the opportunity is you are dealing with. The change in your attitude can bring about change in others (New You is A Powerful YOU). We have to sharpen our minds and rethink our thoughts.

The enemy can sniff out the weakness of your mind and, if you are not equipped for battle, you will be defeated. You have to learn the power of prayer and positive thinking.

For me, prayer changed my life and gave me a source to battle the negative thoughts in my mind. The more I read the word of God and surrounded myself with positive images, the more I was able to alter my thinking. The enemy is not always Satan, nor is the enemy always someone in our circle. Most of the time, we are our own worst enemy.

We control all of what our mind is allowed to do. Just because you think something, does not mean you have to act on it. Think of something else. You have options. Think the opposite of negative thoughts.

See what happens when you do. It cannot hurt. Force yourself to be the person you desire to be. This begins in your thoughts.

Find examples of turning pressure into power to make diamonds instead of confusion and regretted decisions. Turn to the Bible and other sources of positive reinforcement.

The mind is too complicated and too powerful to not appreciate the full capacity of it. Use it to your benefit. The mind is a tool that should be sharpened daily with new knowledge.

Remember everything will sound right to you if you do not know better. So your job is to know better. I began to sharpen my mind with positive reading, relying on the word of God, and surrounded myself with people who were living a blessed life. I also joined groups outside of church that were providing knowledge about healthy mental and physical lifestyles, community growth, and entrepreneurship.

The enemy will never be able to filter your thoughts if you are equipped and know when the enemy is on attack. And just so you are on permanent notice: The enemy is ALWAYS on attack.

But, if your thinking involves God and positivity, the enemy has no chance.

Do not be conformed to the ideologies of the world, your friends, your family, or what the media says is normal. Outside sources will filter your thinking and we have to constantly transform our thinking in order to stay positive and think positive.

After dealing with the daily pressures, we have to renew our minds. Since we have no choice but to reenergize, why not think positive thoughts? There are some people who reenergize by using negative thoughts to influence their drive. Leave negativity out of the picture. You do not want to base a positive on a negative. They cancel each other out. Build your growth and foundation from positivity. Your end result will be worth it. No matter how you look at life there is a glass half full in everything we experience. You just have to find it. Each new rising of the sun brings forth new opportunity to sharpen our minds and become wiser. Each new rising of the sun also gives us a chance to learn from our mistakes, apologize for our wrongs, and increase our minds and our territories. Your future is in your thinking.

Our minds control how we live, the way we interact with friends, family, coworkers, and strangers. Do you remember the old folks saying, "I woke up this morning with my mind on Jesus?"

Just these simple words reminded them that God was ordering their steps. They were allowing God's will to be done by accepting His grace. How could they not be positive?

We tear ourselves down before we even step out of bed. I remember I used to go to bed, and still do sometimes, thinking about what I have to think about the next day. Are we thinking too much or are we thinking about the wrong things?

Ever gone to bed and awakened the next morning only to still be thinking about what you went to bed thinking about? For whatever reason, you are stuck in the day before. If you let go of whatever it is, you can open your mind to new thoughts and you can begin to experience new things. If you do not let go, you are already defeated.

Each morning I wake up praying, singing a song, or reading something positive before I place my feet on the floor.

Remember, the moment you wake up, the enemy is already up and waiting. It is like they sniff you out. The phone rings, and it is someone on the other line talking about some mess that happened at work; or a family member calls with some dilemma that only you can help them with, when you are battling your own demons. Your relationship with yourself and your relationship with God will get you through.

A sharp mind must include more than images and a repetition of words. We must live what we think in order for it to have meaning in our lives. If your mind is filled with negative people, places, and things, this cup will run over and spill over into your ability to make rational decisions.

We become our thoughts. If your mind still holds the images of the last time you failed at something, remove it. Holding on to failure can keep you from accomplishing something grand. Each time you attempt something new, the images will flash before you and you will feel defeated in your heart. Learn from failure, remove it from your system, and then accomplish whatever it is you failed and many more goals you were working on.

Nothing in your life will change unless your mind is changed. We have to cast down the negative thoughts and begin to think positive thoughts. You can think about whatever you want to think about. You can convince yourself to do anything you want to do.

You can choose not to think about how many times you failed, how many folks who have never loved you when you loved them, how many times you prayed and nothing happened.

Instead of accepting defeat and settling, you can be resilient. Not resilient until you achieve a victory, but resilient (period).

When you look in the mirror, you see resilience. When others see you, they see resilience. The choice is yours. It's your mind, attitude and future.

Set your mind on living a purposeful life. No longer will you be mad, no longer will you be upset about situations in your life. You do not have to be stuck in your present state.

You have the power to think your way to a better life. You have to make your mind up!!! Be careful what you think.

Mark 4:24 says, "Consider carefully what you hear." He continued: "With the measure you use, it will be measured to you — and even more." Our voices need to be the most influential voice we hear. Speak to yourself and speak positive words to yourself, speak victory over and over again to yourself. Condition your mind to be peaceful and not chaotic.

We are created as thinkers and that is why we have this complicated mechanism called the brain. We have to maintain it and exercise it just as we do our bodies. Healthy minds yield healthy decisions.

"Maintenance of the Soul and Spirit"

Maintenance simply defined is the process of keeping something in good condition. My car comes to mind when I think of keeping something in good condition.

We all know that if routine maintenance schedules are not upheld, our car will not function to its full potential. Likewise, when putting the soul and spirit within this context, the goal is the same.

The soul is crucial to our spiritual health. It is the wealth from which we draw our identity, desires, and emotions. Simply, the soul is the concept of the personality that makes you 'you', the spirit is the aspect of humanity that connects us to God.

To keep our innermost being within its best condition, we must adhere to regular maintenance schedules. Living in the hustle and bustle of life, we can be put in a position where things on the ever impending to-do list can seem impossible to accomplish.

There are deadlines at work, homework to turn in (if you are an adult student like I am), children to care for, bills to pay, and the list goes on and on.

It is all too easy to get lost in the thick of things; however, if we do not take out time solely for ourselves, we are quickly headed into burnout country.

I will never forget when I became a new driver and I was learning all the things required to maintain a car; the mechanic made it clear to me that if any of the red lights come on behind the steering wheel, that it is not a good sign.

He went on to explain these lights serve as a warning that something is wrong. When my soul and spirit are compromised, my light comes on by way of fatigue, stress, and irritability just to name a few.

I know I am off kilter when I pull up to my job with the attitude of nobody better not try me today. I am snappy when I am asked one too many questions by my co-workers and everybody and everything gets on my nerves.

When I show up under these conditions, it is time to pop that hood and address the problem.

I know that the soul and spirit are disconnected when I cannot seem to make it through a day without feeling on edge. I know it is time to regroup when I am less than a pleasure to be around.

As women we tend to wear so many hats, so it is crucial that we take time out to go to our respective corners of the world and get to that quiet space.

We must turn off the phones and computers and get away from the distractions and get to that peaceful place.

The soul and spirit are like your appetite; they must be fed and nourished to fulfillment. Where is your space? How do you feed yours? I first close my eyes and focus on God's face; then I vent until I cannot vent anymore. And last but not least, I search the scriptures for words that I can meditate on throughout the day.

As women, it is of the upmost importance that we find our piece of peace on earth in order to replenish the soul and the spirit back to where we are functioning in tip-top condition.

The soul needs you to get back to you so it is imperative that you find the things and place that provide that ever-so-vital refreshment. The spirit is our connection to God, so regular dialogue must be tentatively scheduled if we plan to run like a well-oiled machine.

We are sure to maintain our hair and nails and have fly outfits. The outward appearance is all in order; but what people do not see is our innermost being which matters most to keep us with the running status of good condition.

Nicole Battle

A caterpillar becomes a butterfly through slow and steady transformation. A girl becomes a woman through the same. It is sometimes necessary to cut yourself off from the world to invest in your future. The end result of your investment will always justify the means and respect for the due diligence in your plan.

Part IV: Empowerment

Empowerment Comes Though Humility

Pillar # 6

Stewardship

"At the end of your life on earth you will be evaluated and rewarded according to how well you handled what God entrusted to you."
Rick Warren

Stewardship is responsible planning and management of resources. Stewardship has been applied in diverse realms dealing in environment, economics, health, property, religion; it is linked to sustainability. The word is also used in a more general way to refer to a responsibility of taking care of something belonging to someone else. How can you give back and benefit those around you while sustaining yourself simultaneously? These two tasks truly can go hand in hand and strengthen each other at the same time.

For starters, you are a better person in general when you put your energy toward investing in yourself. You also become a better person by giving of yourself. Release and therapy can come from interaction with others; hearing others' pain, and releasing yours. On your journey throughout the 9 pillars, it will be your duty to be a steward. Your time, your testimony, your truth, and your experience serve as a resource to influence or be influenced, to be an example of or take away a lesson from, or simply to be an active part in growth. You will find your tank of resiliency constantly on full from the gift of being a steward. Being a steward is an honor.

Being a volunteer is another form of being a steward. Volunteering is a way to help take care of something belonging to someone else. You can volunteer your time and/or you can donate money if your budget allows.

Being a steward usually means tending to land or property. We want you to extend the responsibility to people. You are your sister's keeper. Do not overwhelm yourself as you are a work in progress. Stay in your lane. Sometimes being your sister's keeper is to notice that a word of encouragement is needed and provide that encouragement. You will know. You have looked in the mirror and seen it in yourself many times. You should not have a problem seeing yourself in someone else. There is therapy in lifting burdens. Think about it like this: When you create a moment of clarity, the universe guarantees you a moment of clarity. Lastly, there are the little things. Call it a karma investment. Call it what you want as long as you dial it up every so often, and bless and learn from your pain and growth.

Ride or Die?

When you think of stewardship, what comes to mind?

My first thoughts are of being wise with resources. By definition, stewardship means being a good manager of resources that have either been earned or given to you. In addition, stewardship can also apply to our time, talents and attitudes towards life and others.

If you are anything like me, no one has ever given me anything of value that was free, so everything I obtained has been earned. I work long and hard for the "pennies" I collect. Almost seems unfair.

This is the life I have chosen or the temporary life that has been given to me. When you are a steward, you must learn patience. As travelers of this journey called life, we have a civic duty to be a good manager of all that has been entrusted to us. Patience will be the key to your stewardship. A candle burns slowly; nevertheless, it burns and accomplishes its duty. Think of yourself as a candle in the daytime. If you were lit in the daytime, it had to be for a special reason. The reason is because you are the extra light for those who need it. Your light is special. Those who need it will see it. You are a steward.

Stewardship is a responsibility sometimes taught and often learned one of two ways: easy or hard. My testimony through life is that I learned how to exist, but to not live; how to point out problems, but never offer solutions. Through the school of hard knocks, I learned to be accountable for my resources, time and talents. A lot of decisions I made were due to a level of ignorance. At the moment, it seemed to be the right thing to do. As time passed, I realized it was not the most reasonable choice. In increasing my level of stewardship, I have wasted a lot of time and I have mismanaged some people, places, and things but I have grown – not at the expense of others, but at the expense of little pieces of my soul. Think on this, "Waste your money and you're only out of money, but waste your time and you've lost a part of your life." ~ Michael Leboeuf

Been there? Can you relate?

I want you to take a journey with me. I am seeing a very large hamster wheel. Now, imagine yourself getting on the wheel. One thing you must know is that once you get on, you cannot get off. You are walking at a steady pace and the wheel slowly begins to spin. There are days you feel like going fast and the wheel still goes slowly. There are days when you want to go slowly and the wheel's speed increases regardless of your effort or lack thereof. There are days when you want to get off but you can't because, even if you get off, the wheel of life will continue to spin with or without you. You need to stay on and maintain versus getting off and letting it pass you by or trying to play catch up.

217

Can you see it? Can you relate?

If you are transitioning to be a better steward, starting out can be slow and sluggish. Once you begin to understand the benefits of this position, you can become excited and it can catapult you to the next level. Remember: There are plateaus in growth and everyone sees one. After the initial high, you may hit a plateau and become discouraged because you are not seeing any "right now" evidence of your efforts (immediate gratification in your stewardship). Do not become nonchalant or throw in the towel. Find the energy and strength to try again. Against all that is screaming at you not to do so, do it anyway.

This wheel seems perpetual; however, I want you to understand, you are in control of the wheel – if it moves, when it moves, how fast it moves, if you want to even be on the wheel.

One important fact to remember is that you cannot advance if you are not moving forward or if you are not trying. Your interaction with the wheel is a simple example of trying and your stewardship. You have to realize that you are accomplishing something by simply getting on the wheel putting one foot in front of the other and making the wheel go around. You have to try in order to achieve or manage any result or resource. Did you know that YOU POSITION YOURSELF TO RECEIVE BY FAITH when you try? Faith without effort is dead. Change without adjustment is dead as well. Being a steward can be difficult, even scary. If you do what you have always done, you will always get the same result. In a negative respect, this would be called insanity. Do not be insane, choose to get on the wheel and be blessed in your stewardship.

Leslie Barnett

Pillar 7

Staying the Course

"Perseverance is not a long race; it is many short races, one after the other."

Walter Elliot

It's important to remember that a relapse is always in one's future. If you can see a lapse for what it is - a temporary problem -, you can be prepared to respond positively. We all have setbacks; one of the keys to long-term success is dealing with these setbacks in a way that gets you back on track quickly. Try to think of a lapse as a learning opportunity, and turn a negative into a positive. At the same time, be PROACTIVE IN PREVENTIVE MAINTENANCE!

- Identify and avoid triggers
- Change habits
- Change associates and significant others
- Change environments
- Know your boundaries

We will face many challenges throughout the cycle of life. You will hear many different opinions and advice on a variety of conundrums. The two things we want you to remember are that success is in planning; and that staying the course is not so much what challenges you face versus how prepared you are for them. You may have heard the old adage it's not where you start; it's where you finish. This is so wrong; motivational, yet WRONG. Life is very much about where you start and finish. You can admit, commit, and submit now or you can wait until later. The earlier you start with due diligence, the more you are prepared for what life throws at you. Staying the course is as much about investing in your education as it is about resilience, strength and bouncing back. Life will present one hurdle after another hurdle. Hurdles are usually spread out, right? Life's hurdles have no space and you will fall/fail at some attempts to maneuver the hurdles. The beauty in maneuvering is to know when to jump and when to use another method to bypass the hurdle. Life is about the end result. Life is simply about how you handle situations you position yourself in, how you handle situations life puts you in, and how you grow from the end results produced from your choices. Staying the course is about vision. Did you plan your course or did someone plan it for you? Was it by circumstance or are you making provision to control your own destiny? Do not be fooled; destiny is planned. It's not a fairy tale path for the enlightened few. It is a design of preparation, time management, hard work, and faith. If you were going to stay on course, one would think that we would have a map. What more is a map than a preplanned route of how to get there? We have to program our mental, physical, and emotional GPS.

Staying the course is important because by the time you have reached this pillar you should have figured out some things about yourself that you want to change. By the time you reach this pillar, you should be working on seeking help or rearranging something in your life that will help you maintain a competent mental, physical, and emotional future.

Weathering the Storm

In the deepest trenches of a storm lies change; not just any change, but a change that demands your soul to shift. The fierce wind and rain are always scary, but the gift that waits is well worth the trials endured. Storms are a part of this human existence. They come in many forms, i.e., more bills than money, work stress, marital struggles, and the list goes on. As soon as you get a grip on one thing, something else rears its head from around the corner.

There isn't a forecast keen enough to predict this storm's location. There isn't a plan solid enough to prepare for this great act of God. When you meet up with this glorious matriarch of nature, you want nothing more but to flee and wish for it to be over. A storm by definition is any disturbed state of an astronomical body's atmosphere. Have you ever been in such a mess that it disturbed your entire atmosphere? The havoc storms cause are sometimes irreversible. The pain they leave once they've passed causes you to stand back and assess the damage in awe and disbelief. The comfort of your daily life is shaken up. You question why such misfortune is in your life. The proverbial line has been drawn in the sand between your former and future states. It's your choice to either pick up the pieces and rebuild or wallow in it.

Why storms you ask; because there is a gift on the inside of you that has to come out. There is a gift that must come forth from you to bless the world. Within the storm's center is the calm also known as the eye. It is referred to as the calm because in a cyclone it's where the lowest pressure occurs. Like the low pressure, God is the calm in the midst of our storms! He will lead you to your destiny by any means necessary. Even if He has to use the fierce rains and winds to aid you into your predetermined space, it shall be done. You – in the comfort that is your life, in the routine, in the well-defined groove – will never progress if not faced with opposition.

When opposition abounds, you must stay the course. I know this is the last thing you want to do, but you need to feel all the elements of the storm. In order for your gift to come to fruition, you must withstand the pain. It's imperative that you hold on and ride the storm out. You are being strengthened for the next phase of your life. Your character is gaining muscle in order for you to be fully operational and effective when you present your gift to the world. Without motivating factors, without your comfort zone being compromised, the course will be useless. So God uses nature to uncover our greatness. When you hear the wind howling loudly, know that it's time to make a move. You may have setbacks, you might get drenched in the rain, you may have to suffer through but a bend in the road is not the end of the road ... unless you fail to make the turn. Stay in it. Stay the course!

Nicole Battle

Here We Go Again

"Here we go again..." For the third time, the man that I love has come into my life and led me on with hopes of a future, only to tell me later he is not ready for a commitment.

The worst part about it was that I enabled his mistreatment of me by inviting him back into my life over and over again.

My bills were piling up, my home was in disarray, I lacked motivation, no career drive, and mental cloudiness; at first I could not see how all the chaos in my life was directly tied to constantly and consistently clinging to a relationship that was not healthy.

Michael and I had been dating for three years with no commitment in sight. I told myself that "commitment" was the only thing lacking. After all, we spent the majority of our time together. We always had fun and kept things adventurous.

The sex was spectacular AND monogamous. And I never gave more than I got ... so I thought. I spent so much time trying to see the good in what we DID have that I was blind to what it was costing me. CLARITY! Peace of mind. Not knowing where things would lead with this relationship exhibited in so many other areas of my life.

Don't get me wrong: I left claiming it was not enough (more than once). I would go for months resisting the urge to call or reach out and touch what was so familiar, so comfortable. But it would only take one call from him and with no questions, no demands, I would fall right back into exactly what I knew I should be running from, less than what I deserved.

Like a light switch, it was suddenly so clear. The man that I loved would never give me the commitment I not only wanted but deserved. Why would he? I did not demand it. I showed repeatedly that I did not have the willpower to say what I meant and truly mean it.

It was not with the ease of a light switch that I accepted I was the one holding myself back. I needed to stay the course of accepting nothing less than I deserved. I needed to change the habit of going back to what was familiar. I had to set boundaries on the people I allowed in my world, as well as for myself.

As soon as I left him (not just physically but also mentally and spiritually), things started to fall into place. New home, promotions at work, energy to keep my surroundings organized were a just a few things that started to change for me.

Neglecting myself and my purpose kept me from attracting what I wanted in the long run. I proved to myself that if I just stay true to my course, I could have everything I want and deserve.

Nicole Battle

Staying the Course

Sustainability is the capacity to endure. Sustainability is the long-term maintenance and improvement of well-being.

Trying is Just the Beginning

It's February 2009, the year was starting off well and I decided to make a career change and go to Culinary Arts School. I started my first term at the end of last year and wanted to be employed in the field.

I was introduced to a restaurant owner who needed help in a bakery. After interviewing and being hired, Kathy gave me a position as a cashier. I really wanted to be in the kitchen but she said for now she would only use me in the peak times.

It was a family-owned business, which had been around about 10 years and had a loyal customer base. The cuisine was Italian and the restaurant was popular for its decorated shortbread cookies. I was excited to be employed by people who had worked hard and saved just as long for their dream.

I was once more maintaining financially and other areas of my life were balanced as well. On weekends I was still preparing and selling desserts, making new friends and business contacts. Sweet Blessings was becoming more of a reality as a business than just my hobby. I began to brand, getting cards and flyers, learning things about business from the small business owners that were in the Kross, The Street Market Place.

Working in the restaurant influenced me to expand on what Sweet Blessings would offer. The restaurant I worked in had a dinner menu, but it was also a soup, sandwich and salad place with a dessert case. Loving Italian cuisine and healthy eating I was in heaven, so what I decided to do was create my own lunch box menu along with my dessert menu.

Here was the first time I had ever experienced how companies really had a need for lunch boxes for different meetings and events or catering.

So now, I began offering sandwiches, salads and wraps with a side of your choice and one of my miniature desserts. I sold at salons and small businesses and acquired a regular route that was paying off.

As a requirement of having my car through the Ways to Work Program, I had to meet with a financial counselor during the duration of the lease of the vehicle. My coach's name was Richard and we met once a week, discussing my budget and if I had kept it or not and why or why not.

He helped me set short and long term goals. He never told me what to do but asked me what was I looking to accomplish and made suggestions on how to meet these goals.

Richard did not discuss finances with me, but other things that were going on in my life like school and the business. He offered ideas on how I could make my business better and the things I should look at for its growth.

[Family] Services of Greater Houston also helped people who were trying to be entrepreneurs through a program called Thrive, by providing financial and other resources through Scores and other programs.

Of course, there are always those things that come to shake the boat when you think you have gotten it all together and on the right track.

My son had been with his dad for a few months and things were not going well at all. His father and I had been in an abusive relationship, so intentionally (or not) I never really allowed him to be a part of his life. It was my way of getting back at him, in a small way.

The reality of it all not only hurt my ex, but my son as well. They both needed the full experience of the father-son relationship to become the men they needed to be for each other.

Not being in his life in his early years to teach him discipline when he needed it the most was a critical error. Needless to say, he was now living in South Park with no real boundaries. This area and lifestyle were totally different than anything he had been used to.

He began to experiment with drugs and was having a hard time in school. He had financial limitations to deal with that he had never realized he had before. Of course I helped as much as I could, but I felt his dad could do more since I had done it all alone for the first 13 years of his life.

I know I had the wrong attitude, but I guess it was due to my underlying hurt. I know having a home where there was enough space for my son and me to coexist in a positive way would have been much better than money.

Even with the limited amount of space I did have being in a one-bedroom, my son wanted to come home. At this point in my life, I was trying to live in a way that honored God as much as possible. I allowed my son to move back home, but I had to make some house rules that I knew would be undesirable to him and made him very aware of what they would be. We transferred him to an alternative school in my neighborhood.

It was mid-October and I received a call saying that my son had been arrested for selling drugs in school. They had taken him to jail and released him on a personal bond, as it was his first offense.

He was now eighteen and spiraling out of control. He had no disciplinary boundaries and had begun to make negative acquaintances.

I admit: I was one of those parents who never went through the bedroom and who took what he had to say at face value. I began to look through his things and found the remainder of the drugs he was selling and a piece of paper with numbers where he had mapped out his profit. OMG!!

My son was not home two days before he had to go back to court. The police picked him up for evading arrest while riding in an unauthorized vehicle.

He went back to jail and got out awaiting sentencing.

It is a hard thing to be a parent knowing that every choice you have made (or not) was a catalyst for these circumstances.

Our relationship had been broken. I loved him more than anything in this life and did not have a clue as to how to communicate it. I was not sure if it would make any difference.

He was my motivation to live a better life, so to know that the life I lived brought us to this place was heart breaking. This is what caused me to realize the only control I have is in my prayer closet.

A mother must seek out every way to be equipped to keep her baby covered no matter what it looks like. This was that season. I began to seek God with everything I had.

As if I was not faced with enough, people from old relationships surfaced right when I was vulnerable enough not to consider why things between us were over with in the first place.

Here I was faced with things that challenged my sustainability; again, my lack of consistency, change and commitment had me feeling the past was not the past. I did not seek help but I knew it was not a challenge I was equipped to face.

It was now 2010 and I decided to see a counselor so I could break the strongholds of dysfunctional relationships in my life, as it pertained to family, friends or a lover.

I know and understand now that doing the same thing over and over and expecting a different result was a sign of insanity.

Before I knew it, I was no longer working in the restaurant; I had a job at a senior living home as wait staff and would work in the kitchen as needed. The hourly pay was not enough to cover my living expenses and the incurred cost of my son being incarcerated.

I was still delivering box lunches on the days I could because I was still attending school. From the outside looking in, you would think I had enough to cover everything because business was good. I was also attracting new contracts.

What I came to discover is that if you do anything, in order for it to work you must have ample knowledge or it will never meet its full potential.

I was wherever someone was trying to eat: Greens Point, Humble and Third Ward. My financial coach was encouraging me to do the things necessary for the success of my business. He wanted me to work smarter not harder because every 'gig' was not worth it.

It was as if I had this hidden fear of numbers and doing the right things that it would take to get me out of financial bondage, not to mention needing to break old habits of not living within my means and emotional spending needed to be over.

Things were falling apart and mid-year I would lose yet another apartment. My son and I moved in with my sister and her family while I continued trying to get my life together.

With all the stressors, including my relationship with my son getting increasingly worse, it seemed as though there was no peace in sight.

I was beginning to break on the inside without even noticing it. Before I really snapped, the year was near its end. I received a job at a new hotel opening in downtown Houston at the beginning of 2011.

The holidays had come and gone and the human resource office of the hotel was calling everyone in to complete paperwork for new hires. On the day of orientation I was so excited and in good spirits. This was the start of something new in my field of choice, on a job where my income would be paying its expected range.

The morning went well but while on a break just before lunch something started happening to me and I did not know what it was. I began to black in and out, as if I was falling asleep uncontrollably and waking up.

That was the beginning of my traumatic mental experience. By the week's end I was in a mental ward. Not knowing or understanding what was happening to me, all I could do was lean and depend on the word of God.

I prayed more and read more of the word of God than I had ever done in my life. Leaving the mental ward after a week, my life and everything in it were still intact – my job, business, and I am of sound mind and body. Glory to God.

So now I live my life with a new awareness of who God is and I can state He is as He was yesterday, today and tomorrow, all present and in control.

Staying the course is not as worrisome or fearful, because I wholeheartedly believe everything works out for my good. Nothing is final and you can always begin again utilizing the lessons learned from past mistakes; they are only teaching tools.

Tangela Russ

A steady drip of water will wear a hole in a rock. The convicted will of one will have effect on many in her path. She will change the world once she knows she can penetrate a rock.

Pillar # 8

Give Back & Pay It Forward

Service to others is the payment you make for your space here on earth.
Mohammed Ali

We have to get to what makes sense and what is tradition. We have become basic by getting away from the basics. We have to get back to producing what our grandmothers produced concerning character, ethics, and patience. We have to recreate the moral fiber that:

- Keeps families together through the toughest of times
- Decreases teen pregnancy and unwed mothers by showing and educating women of their worth
- Creates leaders for our children to follow
- Creates a standard of leading by example in your own household (we have a ways to go … don't expect the movement to start raising your children but definitely expect better examples for them to follow … remember it is a process that starts with you)
- Accepts responsibility for our decisions, health, finances, and religion

- Empowers yourself to see past the day and start planning for the future. We must start being proactive concerning improvement. Stop acting like there is no more tomorrow! You are here now and can do something about it. We have a life to live; why not start living now?

It is Sunday, you have gone to church and given your 10% if you were able. Now it is time to continue giving back. You barely had 10% to give back to the church so what do you give? Give a piece of yourself. To be a pillar in the community, you must invest in where you come from. There are many organizations in your community that can use your help. All you have to do is research these entities and ask. Everyone needs a volunteer. It's up to you. Volunteer where you see the biggest service is needed. Day care centers, libraries, the YWCA, work force centers, jails. Everyone needs help. Cook meals and pass them out where you see the homeless and less fortunate. Be a big sister. See if the elders in your community need any assistance around the property (lawn, trash, and house maintenance upkeep). Your help could be for setting a doctor's appointment or taking someone to a job interview who does not have transportation. People think giving back is only a monetary thing. That is far from the truth. While monetary resources are great, your time, that old suit that you now longer wear, and advice can go a lot further and have a greater impact.

Clenched Fists

Have you heard the saying, "A clenched fist cannot shake hands?" Well, that is not the only thing clenched fists cannot do. When a life is full of self-absorption and selfishness, it cannot be described as being fruitful.

Personally, I have observed countless individuals whose lives are full of promise, possibility, and talent and they are going nowhere fast. These same individuals demand pay for any and every contribution they make, be it small or great. When accolades are given, you'd better not have forgotten to acknowledge them. They appear to have all the "stuff" they need, yet they truly have nothing.

Am I alone in knowing people like this?

The consensus of some people is that "things" equate to prosperity, and because of this some seek for fortune and fame. They seek acknowledgement and demand respect through their prestigious titles because it means they have "arrived."

Do not misunderstand what I am saying. There is nothing wrong with being prosperous, and obtaining fortune, fame, titles, nor wanting respect. The problem comes when we leave humility behind.

My late pastor Jerry Hannon always said, "If you want to be blessed, your fist can't be closed, nothing can come in, and nothing can go out. Strive for better, obtain all the knowledge and understanding life has to offer, move up through the ranks of life, and obtain titles along with all the wealth you can; but don't allow those things to consume you."

Many years ago I worked with a lady I will call Sarah. Sarah was a supervisor in a different department and she walked the planet like she was in total control of everyone. She never spoke a kind word to anyone. It was not unusual to hear her literally yelling at her adult employees like they were children. They lined up like kindergarteners with her at the front of the line going on their morning break. She was relentless for firing hard-working individuals for minor infractions and she would laugh about it in their faces. If you can imagine, Sarah was not a very pleasant person at all. She had built a reputation and was not favored but hated for it.

I am sure Sarah was not at all concerned about her behavior because she had "arrived": she drove the nice car, wore the best clothes, probably had a beautifully made and adorned home; but, one day just as we all broke for lunch, Sarah had an aneurism in the parking lot for all to see. There she lay at the door of her nice vehicle, fist clenched, and to my amazement, it seemed as though 10 minutes passed by and no one moved to assist her. Not the people she worked so hard for, and definitely not the employees she tortured. My supervisor didn't even go and assist her, and if I recall he was CPR certified.

No one cared!! I even heard people laugh and say things like that is what she gets. There was no compassion. I was truly in shock. Not only was a tyrant brought low, but the fact that no one was moved with compassion alarmed me.

I am sure Sarah never would have seen herself in this position. She had money; but, she could not pay anyone to help her. She had made a name for herself; but, instead of it speaking for her, it spoke against her. She had on nice jewelry and even lay at the shaft of a tire on her $50,000 car, but how did any of those "things" help her?

Sarah had long forgotten humbleness; her identity was in all the things that were not prospering her anything. Her fists were clenched; nothing fruitful went out and, unfortunately, nothing fruitful could come in.

In spite of herself, Sarah survived. With much therapy, she finally came back to work a different individual. She smiled at people, and it seemed sincere. She said good morning and was pleasant. Her employees stated she made small talk about their families, something she never did before.

Was it her near death experience that changed her, or was it the fact that during her near death experience, no one came to her aid?

If your fists are clenched, open them wide. It's the only way to be a recipient of blessings.

Leslie Barnett

The Golden Rule

As with anything I set out to do, my first action is to consult God and wait for an answer. Sometimes answers seem to come instantly, and then there are times an answer comes that I do not like and do not want to receive. More often, it would appear that I am in a constant state of waiting for an answer.

I have learned in my waiting that God is trying to teach me a lesson and, while doing so, He is preparing a witness statement for an individual I will soon encounter. At first I was very indignant about this because I was looking at things the wrong way.

No, it does not feel good to go through painful and hurtful situations; however, if you think about what an honor it is to be used by God, it makes the journey seem easier to travel. Once I realized this, I began to recognize what other gifts He has imparted within my life.

From my years as a child through today, I have always been charitable and compassionate. It seems like I could sense another person's pain and I had to do something to help. I often was scolded about this because my family did not understand me. In love, they tried to change who God made me to be but, I am proud to state, to no avail.

I've been called a social butterfly because there is no place that I go that someone does not know who I am. We may not know one another's name, but I am always in place to be used by God should He need me. The way I see it, how can you witness to a person you do not know. Yes, it can be done; however, if you make yourself tangible to people, they are more likely to receive what you have to say.

You see, we are not here for our glory, nor is it about me and mine. Our lives should be to help meet the needs of others, to leave an inheritance that others will see and want to emulate. The golden rule keeps me grounded; it is more blessed to give than it is to receive.

Despite not having a lot, sacrifices are a requirement when we are committed to being selfless. If I were to wait to be rich to be a blessing to someone else, I would never be able to help anyone. Finances are not the only way to be a blessing. We can give time and effort to causes and people. Sometimes, a listening ear is all a person needs.

I admonish you to make a conscious effort to seek opportunities to give back. You may not have a lot; but for what you do have, if God moves upon your heart and you recognize an individual who has a greater need than yours, do as I do and give what you have. You will never miss it. It will come back to you 100-fold.

God gave us two eyes, two ears, and one mouth. Be swift to see and hear and slow to speak. Don't be so consumed with yourself; take time to notice those who are around you.

You would be surprised what you may hear and see. Weed through the gossip and hear the hurt another may bear. Offer your testimony as a word of strength. When you make lunch, pack an extra sandwich or bring an extra $5 and buy someone's lunch. Because they are working like you, you do not know what they may be facing that prevents them from being able to do so. Offer a smile and say good morning, even if no one else says a word.

Be guilty of bringing sunshine with you everywhere you go! Darkness cannot stand when there is light. Change the atmosphere when you enter a place. It is blessed because you are there! Seek to first please God, and everything else will fall into place.

Recognize by being a blessing to others, you are helping yourself to not only avoid going through trials, but to come out of some things you may be facing.

As with anything, there are those who will try to take advantage of you. Don't allow it to deter or discourage you from your newfound purpose. Seek God for understanding and exercise wisdom, and He will order your very steps.

As women we must give back to our future, our community, and to ourselves. Too often we are tight-lipped with information thinking that someone will be more successful than we were with it. STOP THIS NOW! We must realize that society will only grow as much as we nourish it. As much as we invest in ourselves. As much as we set the standards. We can only nourish it by sharing knowledge. Education and knowing better are key with a society that is wealthy in health, family, religion, relationships, finances, and vision. We are as only as strong as the team we build around us. We are only as strong as our weakest link. By networking and networking, we build a society that is based on sisterhood and support. Support is so necessary because we all have and will need to confide in, talk to, laugh with, and HELP one and other. This is bigger than me. This is bigger than you. This is bigger than us, but collectively we can do it.

Leslie Barnett

If you leave a piece of you with everyone you come in contact with, you will change the world to be a better place by the mere miracle of your existence. Value your existence. Know your worth and value your worth. You are not here by chance. You have endured trials and tribulations to be a testimony. You are a defining page in someone else's book. You are here to share your story. You are light at the end of the tunnel and others need to know that that glimmer far off in the distance is a reality, they can do it and you are the example of getting it done.

Pillar # 9

Commitment

Focus, Foresight, and Flexibility = Success
Rickie Chaffold

I am Me. In the entire world, there is no one else exactly like me. Everything that comes out of me is authentically mine, because I alone chose it – I own everything about me: my body, my feelings, my mouth, my voice, all my actions, whether they be to others or myself. I own my fantasies, my dreams, my hopes, my fears. I own my triumphs and successes, all my failures and mistakes. Because I own all of me, I can become intimately acquainted with me. By so doing, I can love me and be friendly with all my parts. I know there are aspects about myself that puzzle me, and other aspects that I do not know – but as long as I am friendly and loving to myself, I can courageously and hopefully look for solutions to the puzzles and ways to find out more about me. However I look and sound, whatever I say and do, and whatever I think and feel at a given moment in time is authentically me. If later some parts of how I looked, sounded, thought, and felt turn out to be unfitting, I can discard that which is unfitting, keep the rest, and invent something new for that which I discarded. I can see, hear, feel, think, say, and do. I have the tools to survive, to be close to others, to be productive, and to make sense and order out of the world of people and things outside of me. I own me, and therefore, I can be me. I am me, and I am Okay.

– Virginia Satir

A Rule for Life

Making a commitment to yourself can be a difficult challenge to accomplish. We are constantly taking care of everything accept ourselves.

To whom much is given much is required ... we are constantly nurturing the kids, the job, the bills, the husband, the house, the boyfriend, the in-laws, and the list could go on and on.

If one seriously wants change, one has to pull oneself out of the madness and do a self-evaluation of your particular situation.

Ask yourself these questions:

1) What is my purpose?

2) Am I happy with my life, and what do I need to do to improve it?

3) Do I have a plan ... a family plan, a professional plan ... a "me" plan?

4) Are my spirit, mind, and body healthy?

You have come through 8 pillars and you have ended up here. Commitment is your beginning and your never-ending quest to hold it together. You will be blessed and cursed. You will face trials and tribulations. You are human and are not exempt from the joys and pains of your actions. You have consequences and commitment is a safe guard to effectively put standards of accountability in perspective. You must begin your journey with commitment and you must stay the course with your commitment. This commitment is not a New Year's resolution, but instead a life-forming, habit-changing, spirit-filled, I-am- ready-to-make-a-change commitment. The most important single factor in individual success is COMMITMENT. Commitment ignites action. To commit is to pledge yourself to a certain purpose or line of conduct.

The most important single factor in individual success is COMMITMENT. Commitment ignites action. To commit is to vow yourself to a plan, purpose, and goal that must remain as flexible as Murphy's Law. If the plan fails, change the plan not the goal. You hold yourself to a standard, a line of conduct. Commitment also means practicing your beliefs consistently. Your commitment has a great deal to do with you being accountable. Your commitment is secured with two basic fundamentals. You must have a sound set of beliefs to be committed to and you must find the faith of one believer within your actions and behavior. Possibly the best description of commitment is "Non-deterred determination."

Being a Pillar in the Community

1. Selfless

2. Compassionate

3. Patient

4. Respected

5. Mother

6. Wife

7. Friend

8. Steward (work and other's people's existence)

9. All women in one

If you are 1, 2, 3, 4, you will have no problem being 5, 6, 7, 8, and 9.

You will find that you have small characteristics of all of these traits in you. We have to get back to what makes sense and the balancing of evolution and what is traditional. We have gotten lost in the present by not preparing for the future. We have to get back to acting like Madea or Meme. We have to recreate the moral fiber that:

1) Keeps families together through the toughest of times

2) Decreases teen pregnancy and unwed mothers by showing and educating women of their worth

3) Creates leaders for our children to follow

4) Creates a standard of leading by example in our own household (We have a way to go ... do not expect the movement to start raising your children but definitely expect better examples for them to follow ... remember, it is a process that starts from within)

5) Empowers to see past the day and start planning for the future. Too many of us are not looking and planning for the future. Stop acting like there is no more tomorrow and start acting like better days are coming; better days yet are here.

We have one life to live and we are about to start living by accepting responsibility over our existence.

The Other Side of Through

I have been going through a great trial for almost four years now. I could have very well given up. I could have allowed my mind to tell me that my present state would be my future situation and there was no need to think differently.

I have been unable to walk without a walker since March 12, 2008. I have been struggling in my mind to stay focused on positive things and to believe that I am going to get off this walker.

I am in a constant battle with my thoughts and the enemy who whispers things like, "You will never walk again, you should just sit in your wheel chair and relax. They will push you around. You will never get better. You too fat to walk, so just eat and enjoy." I refuse to listen to his words.

For a long time, I truly believed it all and woke up every day the same way. Unable to walk, no hope and I had just given up.

One day, I got tired of waking up the same way that I went to bed. Hopeless, I asked God to do what He said He would do. Never leave me nor forsake me. I need you to know that I am your child and that defeat is not an option.

I began to read the word of God, I began to sing a song daily, and I began to wake up with my mind on Jesus. I would literally tell myself that I am not thinking that way today. I will not be defeated.

If I made one step today, maybe I can make two steps tomorrow. I also spoke victory over my situation.

Once the Word was in my heart, the images of defeat began to dwindle away, though it was a great struggle.

I begin to pray and say, "God, You said if I dwell in You, I can ask You what I will. Help me to think positively and believe that I can move these limbs. Be my body, because I am too weak, Lord. I know that you are stronger than I am." Once I got my mind, body and soul in sync, I began to think like a walking person again. I began to think positively and I had what I needed to battle Satan who dwelled in my thoughts.

The more I sharpened my mind with God's words, with holy songs, and positive thoughts, Satan fled.

I am stronger now than I have ever been. I can take a few steps without my walker and I am now able to think my way through doing something different each day.

My mind has been changed. Transformation brings forth determination. I am determined to serve God and to do His will. My mind has been cleansed of negative thoughts.

There are still days that I feel like I just cannot make it. But, I am equipped now and know how to battle those thoughts. I grab the word of God and I read it out loud. I listen to a song that encourages me to go on. I sing out loud so that I can hear the words of the lyrics.

God has made me whole and I call on Him when I need Him. Restoration of the mind gives you peace. As you go through trials and tribulations, you have to stay positive. You have to maintain a sharp mind full of positivity.

During your wait, you have to keep your mind sharp and ready for the enemy. No one knows the time or day God will show up and deliver, but you better be ready and stay that way.

Preparation for restoration is the key. Ask God to give you the patience to wait and the courage to continue to move forward in your walk. Your mind has to be prepared to carry you through your preparation. Maintenance of the mind is important to your restoration.

To change your life is to change your mind.

Chandra Daniels

Family Plan

Family is a forward moving catalyst to realize and embrace nurturing. Nurturing is a must that women have to get back to as it pertains to family. You are the first teacher. You are the original teacher. Women have to reinvest and start taking an equal stance of 'I am the Head and not the Tail' mentality as it relates to the children, relationships, household, and growth.

Women must follow their hearts to the end of their ignorance and begin making heartfelt decisions that incorporate facts and God.

We are in a State of Emergency that is characterized by HIV, teen pregnancy, low graduation rates, unprecedented incarceration, domestic violence and a lack of trust and interaction with the church and government.

We must step up to the plate of change and accept our roles in life.

We all live for family to some degree. We want our parents and grandparents to be proud of us. We want to impress our brothers and sisters. We want to grow up and have a family ... not just a family, but a functional family. We want our children to look at us, follow our example, and respect us.

All of the above requires the nurturing and managing of collective and individual relationships. This management raises the nurturing bar to another degree. This particular management involves nurturing to make the people, attitude, energy, and environment around you better so that you can be a better you.

Nurturing is wisdom to know that there will always be strength in numbers, family, and community. It is the inner feeling to know that we all need somebody and know the difference between sincere and false interactions placed in your life.

Being a Mother

Raise your hand if you have the characteristics of Madea, Me Ma, MiMi and whatever other nicknames that you have been given as grandma:

1) Giver of life
2) Matriarch of the family
3) Disciplinarian (will discipline other children, too)

4) Philosopher

5) Pillar in family and community (who is respected by everyone)

6) Healer

7) Cheer squad

8) Voice of reasoning

9) There when no one else is

10) Visionary

Being a Wife

Raise your hand if you have the characteristics of what a man considers a good wife:

1) Life coach

2) Friend

3) Support

4) Not argumentative but instead solution driven

5) Visionary

6) Excellent parenting skills

7) Being a good business partner (marriage is a business)

8) Knowing when to give space (space is relevant for growth of both beings)

9) Humor

10) Communicator

11) Secure with oneself and the relationship

Cocktails and Words of Wisdom

It was 'Girls Night Out' and I was so happy to be surrounded by two of my closest girlfriends, Dawn and Kendra. The ladies and I made it our business to get together once a month to simply chill out while expressing our feelings about our current issues of life and love.

While leaving the children and men at home, the girls and I embarked on enjoying a couple of hours of freedom and necessary "ME TIME." As usual, we met at the local steak and seafood house for cocktails and laughter.

"Hey ladies, guess who is in engaged?!?," shouts Dawn as she flashes a beautiful pear shaped diamond ring. "OMG," I scream. "Congrats," says Kendra as she happily claps her hands. "We are so happy for you, girl!"

"Have you guys set a date yet?," I ask with excitement. "I know we are in this wedding!" "Of course you are – cannot get married without my girls. We have not set an exact date yet," replies Dawn.

"Michael and I are thinking about a summer wedding. I am so happy and so nervous!"

"Why nervous?," I ask her. Dawn pauses and says, "I love Michael very much and I want to spend the rest of my life with him. I am just nervous about being a good wife because I want to make him happy and be everything he needs me to be."

"Dawn, sweetie you cannot make someone happy all the time, nor can you be everything he needs you to be all the time. There is no such thing as perfection. That only exists in fairytales."

Kendra joined the conversation. "The key to having a successful and lasting marriage is understanding your role as a wife, understanding your mate, and keeping God first," she deeply explains.

"Really, that's all it takes," Dawn replies sarcastically. "You make it sound so simple." "It is simple - it's so simple that it's complicated," she responds.

"If you understand your role and communicate, the easier it is. Take it from me: Jamal and I have been married seven years. It has been a good seven, but we have had some rocky moments too. Majority of those rocky moments were caused by lack of communication, and not fulfilling our promises to God and each other."

She continued, "Your role as a wife is to be a helpmate, the emotional support system for your husband and your family. In order for you to be what Michael needs and wants, you have to know what those wants and needs are. The two of you have to be on the same page. He cannot be the Cliff Huxtable Cosby Show type husband and you are the Erica Kane All My Children type of wife. Those two are a crazy combination destined to fail."

"Dawn, I totally agree with Kendra when she says understanding and knowing your mate is important. Sometimes as women we tend to have unrealistic expectations and those unrealistic expectations can cause hurt feelings and a rift in your marriage. If your man was not romantic when you were dating, do not expect candlelight dinners, love poetry, and flowers for no reason once you guys tie the knot. We always want to be accepted for how we are but are so quick to try and change them." Dawn and Kendra laughed.

"So, my role as a wife is to be a helpmate," questions Dawn. "Yup," I reply. "Helpmate means being there through thick and thin, giving moral support, being his cheering section, good listener, motivating him, and the list continues."

"Being a good wife is a job, sweetie, and it is hard work, with tons of dedication. When I told my grandmother that Ryan and I were getting married, the first thing out her mouth was make sure he always has a hot meal waiting for him and that he comes home to a clean house. If you do those things, your husband will always be happy.

Well, in my household Ryan does the cooking and we have a housekeeper that keeps the house in order. So it takes more than cooking and cleaning to make a healthy marriage.

Being a wife is much more than being a personal chef, washing clothes, dusting, and cleaning. Do you guys remember my friend, Michelle?"

"Yes," answers both Dawn and Kendra. "What about her?," questions Kendra. "Well, Michelle is the poster child for how to be a successful woman. On the outside, it seemed like she had the picture perfect life. She owns her own business. She is pretty, talented, driven – and does not have a clue on how to maintain a relationship.

She was so focused on her career that she did not spend any time with her husband. When she was not working late hours, she was out of town or out with her friends.

Michelle was so focused on her own professional endeavors that she treated her husband as if he was an afterthought. At one point her husband lost his job and she used that as an opportunity to belittle him. Every time he tried to talk to her about the lack of respect and quality of time she displayed towards their marriage, she would blow him off.

She felt that he was jealous of her success and that he needed to focus more on his own professional career. Michelle felt as long as she was faithful, paid some of the household bills, and occasionally gave him sex she was doing her duties as a wife.

Eventually, they got a divorce. After the divorce, she ended up dating this guy. And after he took her on a rollercoaster ride of heartache and pain, she realized what a good man her ex-husband was.

The sad thing is she does not see anything she did wrong in the marriage. She feels like she did everything she was supposed to do as a wife."

After ordering another round of drinks from the passing waiter, Dawns says, "That is sad. If you do not realize the mistakes you made, you are going to repeat them again and again. Sometimes it seems like we value being a professional success more than being a good wife. We can have it all, the successful career and a healthy strong marriage." "Yes, we can," I tell her. I want to make a toast.

We each lift our glasses and I say, "To Dawn loving your husband the way he deserves and doing so without sacrificing your own happiness. Love him with intense passion and respect him with no boundaries. Never be the reason he questions his manhood and never treat him like all he is to you is a paycheck. I wish you a lifetime of happiness. Know your role as a wife and play it well."

Cheers!

Contrina Jenkins

Professional Plan

The professional you will be a hard subject to address as well. This next step is crucial once we have forgiven, embraced, and started loving ourselves. We must create a plan. This plan first starts with:

1) Knowing who you are
2) Assessing where you are at in life
3) Realizing if you are happy with work and family
4) Acting on the answer to the previous question whether the answer is positive or   negative
5) Deciding who stays and who goes

Growth is going to allow you an opportunity to let people, relationships, girlfriends, boyfriends, ideas, and thoughts GO! Growth is also going to allow you an opportunity to let God and your vision increase your territory.

Yes, your growth will be the beginning of a health, mental, and emotional diet.

This is the first day of the rest of your life, and this beginning cannot afford to be wasted again.

We must embrace **PMA** ... Positive Metal Attitude and release **ANT** ... Always Negative Thinking.

Collateral Damage

Kemberley was young, opulent and unique. She was the first and only one in her family to graduate from college. She secretly stripped to make ends meet.

Seven years later she made it, and the fruit of her hard work placed her in the spotlight. She had it all: the title, the job, the position, big house, the car. She had status, but for some reason she was missing something.

She was the first and only one to "make it" and that fact put a strain on her family relationships. Some were happy for her but others were jealous. "She thinks she's better than us now."

It is amazing that bettering yourself can upset the mindsets of those content in their own dysfunctional decisions. She used to let this bother her, but soon came to the realization that it was a waste of positive energy to entertain such madness.

More so, she realized that she had more to focus on and the successful life she was currently living. She was single and yearning for a relationship. She lived in a gated community where everyone was married. It was the quintessential American dream. The community was made up of houses with white picket fences, one-car garages, children (a boy and a girl) and a pet.

She witnessed this day in and day out. It did not make her sad, but it definitely made her want more out of life. She admired the couples and their happiness. She also admired the bigger houses. She longed for the day when it would be her walking in one of those bigger houses with a family and a pet.

She was not accepted but still tried to fit in. She came to all the town hall meetings and tried to make a few friends. She befriended a few but was still shunned by the rest. Guess it was the fear of what a roaming or bored husband might do that kept the ladies from being their friendliest.

She did, however, befriend one special lady that changed her outlook on life and relationships.

Let's call her Jane. Jane was the middle class, stay-at-home wife. She had the big house, two-car garage, nanny, a husband and kids.

One day while driving by, she pulled up to Jane's driveway to say hi. Jane was unloading some groceries into the house. The "hi" turned into an invitation to come in.

Jane with her Gucci shades and her Gucci purse sat down and got settled. They began discussing life and Jane began to cry. "What's wrong?," Kemberley asked. "I have all of this yet I have nothing," Jane responded. "Well, what do you mean? It looks like you're doing pretty well."

Jane said, "I have no life. I have no intimacy. My life is raising my kids and they both graduate this summer. Stedman and I are not intimate and things are rough right now. He has taken on the burden of supporting us and I think he is regretting his choice for me to be a stay-at-home mom. His choice? Yes, his choice. When I first got pregnant, he almost insisted that I stay at home and not work and that took on a life of its own. The frustration that I now feel from it is unbearable and I cannot take it anymore. I want to leave but I can't. I am financially dependent on him. I have no skills. I have no education. I have no will. I have NO life. I am collateral damage."

Now Kemberley was wondering where all this was coming from and when Jane took off her Gucci shades to reveal a black eye, she knew.

Jane had had enough and was reaching out for help. Ironically, Jane picked the one person to release to that was not like her, as she knew. Many women in that community were in some way in the same boat of dysfunction that she was in.

As Kemberley tried to console Jane, a car pulled into the drive way. He's home. She puts back on her Gucci shades and gives me a hug and escorts me to the door. I told her, "I will be in touch with you and will be praying for you."

Neal walks by and does not speak and goes directly into the house. I heard him say, "Where's my dinner? What did you do today? Fix me a drink ..." as the voices faded away and the door slams.

Kemberley was taken aback as she get in her car. She was admiring the relationship, big house, the Gucci, the cars, the kids and realized at the end of the day it meant nothing because this was an eye opening example of someone who had it all and beyond a reasonable doubt was still miserable mind, body, and soul.

This lesson, this encounter gave Kemberley an appreciation for her planned path and her due diligence. She still wanted a relationship but was not willing to rush into things or settle like she might have done before.

She now saw the bigger picture than just having a void filled or the other side of the bed warmed. As she prayed for Jane that night, she thanked God for protecting her mind, body, and soul in a way that allowed her to continue on her path.

She eventually moved out of that community. Her patience and faith led to her to meeting the man of her "dreams." In reality, he was just a simple man who made her happy.

She bypassed being Collateral Damage by sticking to her guns, believing in herself when no one else did, and the desire to want more for herself.

Don't become Collateral Damage!

Collateral Damage

n. Unintended damage, injuries, or deaths caused by an action; is damage to people or property that is unintended or incidental to the intended outcome

Being a Friend

(To your mate, friends, and yourself)

1) Be a leader and not a follower
2) Listen
3) Set good examples
4) Practice what you peach
5) Balance tough love and inspirational acceptance
6) Being there
7) Not taking friendship for granted
8) Being a blessing
9) Allowing friend's mistakes; being the maturity tool verses I told you so's
10) Allow friends to be genuine and allowing yourself to do the same

Outgrowing Your Peers

The ladies decided this "Girls Night Out" will be a sleepover. We usually would go out to a club but no one wanted to spend any money so we stayed in. We all decided it would be a great time to get to know more about each other. Jasmine, Kelly, Crissy and myself (Lauren) have been friends since elementary school and now we are seniors in high school.

We practically knew everything about each other, so we thought, but now it was more. Crissy brought up the idea of telling each other something we did not know about one another.

I was all for it because I had just gotten some good news and wanted to tell them. Crissy went first; she said she wasn't going to college. She felt it was a waste of time. She said she was ready to live her life and school was not going to let her do that.

While getting up Kelly said, "Well, I'm not either. Don't look at me crazy but I am pregnant." Crissy said, "Dang, Kelly, how you spring something like this on us? How far along are you?"

She said, "About three months; but I am going to wait another week before I take a test." At this moment, I knew I wasn't going to be able to share with them what I had planned to do.

I mean after going through who is the dad, are they staying together, Crissy's reasons for not going to college and Jasmine topping it off with her boyfriend being in jail again:

I am sitting at the end of the bed shocked at what my girls had been hiding.

I thought we were getting ready to say what we were going to do next year. Plans to go off to college but they have been doing other stuff.

I wanted to tell them so badly about my acceptance letter to college. It just seemed as if that was not going to happen. I thought we were on the right course. We always talked about going to college and pledging together.

How we were going to become successful in our careers, get married, have children and travel together. It seemed as if I was the only one who was doing things to achieve the goals we had set together.

Now, how am I going to move on without my girls? While sitting on the floor in a daydream about these things, I get snapped out of it by Jasmine asking, "Lauren what do you have to say?"

I said, "Well, I got accepted into college. I will be leaving at the beginning of the summer. I do not understand what happened." Kelly asked, "What do you mean? I said, "We said we were going to college together. You all said things were going well in your classes and you all were ready. I guess I was the only one doing what we said. I mean I love y'all, but this is some crazy stuff."

"So, none of y'all going to college?"

They shook their heads no. I was shocked and had nothing to say for the rest of the night. They finished the night off talking about what was Kelly going to do if she is pregnant and Jasmine leaving her boyfriend.

I just sat there thinking how I am going to go off to college without knowing anyone? What will I do if I need to talk to someone? That night I did not sleep but the next day I left thinking I have to do this for me. I cannot stay here with them. I must go to college. I came into high school without knowing anyone and left knowing everyone. I hope it is the same way when I get to college, because I am going.

Niisha Lewis

I Am Every Woman

Buzzzzz!!! The sound of the 4 a.m. alarm that wakes Kem each weekday morning. She reaches over to hit the snooze button in hopes to steal just five more minutes, but she is well aware that extra sleep is not an option. Kem is scheduled to be at her job at 6:30 am, but her work begins much sooner than that.

As the 27-year-old mother of five rolls out of bed, her only focus is making sure her family is taken care of before she exits the door.

The O'Neals are not your typical Cosby family; they are more like The Brady Bunch meets Good Times.

When Kem met her husband five years ago, she had two daughters from a previous marriage, he had one son from a previous relationship, they legally adopted his nephew, as well as having a two-year-old son together.

The family resides in what they feel is their dream home, a 1600 sq. ft. flat, that they had built the year before. Jay, Kem's husband, works as a regional truck driver for a local distribution center, and Kem works full time as a Surgical Technologist and is a part-time nursing student.

Kem wakes up before the family to get a head start on their day. She cooks breakfast each morning for them because she will not depend on the schools to make sure they are fed.

As she cooks breakfast, simultaneously she is preparing lunches for her husband and their kids. The night before, she makes sure all uniforms are laid out in order, and double checks each morning to ensure everything is ready. Experience has taught her that preparation is the key to success in a high capacity home.

Breakfast has been made, and all plates have been prepared. Each family member has an assigned plate color so that there would never be any confusion as to whom each plate belongs to and who did not clean up after they were done.

It is now 5:30 a.m., and Kem has prepared breakfast, lunch, showered, and is on her way to work. As she drives towards the Texas Medical Center, this is her personal time with GOD.

She lowers the radio and has her daily conversation, praying for the protection and prosperity of her family and friends. She arrives at work at 6:15 am, but her job at home is not yet done.

She gives her husband a personal wake-up call to make sure he and the kids are eating and getting ready for their day. One by one, she gives each child their personal, "I love you", and wishes her husband a great day.

Three years ago, Kem was appointed Lead Technician in her operating room. The skills it takes to maintain her household are the same skills required to manage her team. She is responsible for assigning rooms and making sure the patients and surgeons are happy and cases are being done.

By midday, when most employees are sitting around chatting about their day, Kem does not have that option; this is her study time. As a part-time nursing student, it is critical for her to study hard and make good grades.

While it takes an average nursing student aspiring to obtain an Associate Degree in Nursing only two years, Kem has accepted the fact that it will take her nearly four years because of her part-time status and her home responsibilities. (Sometimes you have to sacrifice what you want in order to take care of what you need to.)

It is now 3:30 and Kem is off of work, but her work is still not done. It is still early, so she is blessed to avoid traffic as she transforms from dedicated employee to chauffer.

At 27, a Ford Astro van is not what she imagined driving, but it is the perfect vehicle for what her life requires. The children are picked up from school and have time enough for a brief wardrobe change and snack before heading to practice.

The boys, ages 6 and 9, have football practice and the girls ages 4 and 10 have cheerleader practice, as Kem must gather all information for an upcoming fund raiser that she plans to share with the other parents, because it is her responsibility as the team mom. Her husband will pick up the 2-year-old at daycare and meet them at practice.

The meeting was a success, all parents are on board, and the O'Neals are headed home. As they arrive home, no instructions are given because the children already know the routine: it's bath time.

As the children take their baths, dad bathes the baby and Kem is preparing their dinner. No fast food or meals from a box; her Louisiana ancestors taught her it does not take much time if you put in enough effort.

Tonight's menu is baked chicken, rice, corn and green beans (because Grandma said you always had to serve something green), accompanied by red Kool-Aid.

As the dinner simmers, Kem gives attention to the youngest of the tribe, as dad takes a hot bath she prepared for him as he dressed the baby.

The table is set, and the family dines together. No television or telephone interruptions, as this is the most valuable time of her day. She gets to hear from each child what they learned and how their day went, while she and her husband enjoy the excitement of their accounts. Dinner is complete and the children take initiative to clear the table as Kem gets a few minutes to unwind, relax and take a hot shower before her hat changes from chef to teacher.

The kitchen is cleaned and the children are at the table doing their homework. They put in so much effort because they are aware of the importance of good grades in the O'Neal household. A structured family is a learning family. If most parents would eliminate video games, television, and computers from their children's daily regimen, they would see a major improvement in their academics.

Children are vessels of what we contribute. A parent should not expect more from a child that they are not willing to sow into.

It's 9:30 p.m. in the O'Neal household, all homework has been checked and the children are tired and ready for bed.

The boys go to their room and the girls to theirs, the baby is alone in his crib, and the Mr. and Mrs. retire to their very own sanctuary. It is important for a married couple to set aside time each day to communicate without any distractions from anything and anyone.

Communication and one-on-one intimacy are very much needed when life has you on a constant schedule. Sexual needs are prevalent with both parties and it is important to maintain a mutual satisfaction. With a big family, busy career, and worldly responsibilities, it easy to get lost in transition.

This is a typical week in the O'Neal household, except on the Tuesdays and Thursdays Kem has classes and her husband takes complete control.

Wednesdays they attend Bible study and the children have choir practice. They have agreed as parents that, if they keep the children busy, they will have no time to get into trouble.

The weekends are just as busy. The children have their games, dad takes the boys for haircuts and Kem takes the girls with her shopping. This is the time when the children receive their gender bonding.

Kem sets aside some personal time later with girlfriends, just to maintain a social balance, because she knows that Sunday evenings belong to the guys.

The need for outside adult conversation is very important because it promotes a healthy mental health and decreases stress.

Sundays are the days when the family takes it easy. Together they visit church, then it's Sunday dinner at either of their parent's homes. This routine rotates to give the children equal amounts of time with other family members. Sunday evenings are not so busy, because this is the day the family prepares for the week.

As the family enjoys a little freedom, Kem makes sure that all laundry is done and her family has everything they need to do it all over again. For many years I asked myself, if I had to do it all over again would I? Each time, the answer remains the same, "Yes", without hesitation.

Deana Benton

Do you want to speak to the man of the house or the woman that runs everything? From the beginning of time, a woman has been in control of monetary order and budgeting. It was like that back then with a two-fold house and it is like that now with single parent run households. The key is simply living within our means and exercising discipline. Planning, saving, and mistakes will come with this growth and way of life. The mistakes will give you a testimony of self of the right way and wrong way for you. You are going to want to get those pair of shoes and think about it for a few days. You decide to get them and put off taking care of priorities. No worries – the bill will come with a final notice next month. It's funny that next week you did not plan for the transmission to go out, but here we are stranded on the side of the highway needing a tow truck and a new transmission. Do we have AAA? Do we have insurance that affords us a rental while transmission is being fixed? Now there is the fork in the road – pay the final notice on the late electricity or get to work ... get that transmission fixed. You cannot return those shoes because you already wore them. Now the struggle begins. Nothing got put off this month except for saving for life's unexpected circumstances. Be sure to include life in your daily plans. I am not saying that you should not spoil yourself ever now and then. I am saying make sure necessities are paid off first and you have an emergency plan. Pay God, pay yourself, pay your bills, and put something in emergency savings. Look at the free money segment attached.

Embracing YOU ... Womanhood

Understanding your worth embarks during childhood. It is a foundation that your parents must provide to you while under their care. I was afforded the opportunity to experience worthiness as a child and a young girl growing up.

My father always made sure that he deposited positivity and uplifting statements of sheer truth into my soul. I was always told how beautiful and smart I was. He would always make sure that he spent time investing irreplaceable morals and standards in me.

As I grew up and began to date, he would always tell me to demand the best from a gentleman. "If he cannot treat you like the princess you are, then he does not deserve you. He must always respect you" is what my dad would always tell me.

Sometimes when a guy would come to the house to take me out on a date, my dad would stand at the door to make sure that the guy would open the door for me, and if he did not my dad would yell out to me, "Dee, you have to demand the best, he needs to open the door for you." Sometimes I would be embarrassed, but my dad only wanted the best for me. He wanted to make sure that the foundation that he built was free of dilapidation.

He wanted me to understand that I was worth being treated like no other female that they had dated prior to me. He reminded me that I was, and am still to this day, a rare and timeless jewel.

To come into contact with someone like me is an experience that is unforgettable and without a doubt must be handled with care and gracefulness.

Time passes on, and I am now excited about being a young lady in college and having a male companion that has swept me off my feet. I was his world, he said all of the right things, and made me feel like nothing I had ever experienced before.

I was naive and green. He began wooing me with what he could do for me. I could identify with that because my dad did nice things for me, and I knew he loved me, so naturally I thought this guy must really love me. I believed everything he said to me, and I would always tell people, "He would never cheat on me."

He would always say how great my passion was and how it was the best ever. I believed him and assumed that I was even more worthy since he felt this way.

He thought I was smart and beautiful and he loved the very essence of my touch and the feeling he got from my physical indulgence that he adored so much.

He exemplified all of the qualities of my father and I was easily his prey. It was not long before the vulture attacked and devoured what I thought to be true.

Situations occurred that turned my world completely upside down. Because of him, I had a vivid and firsthand experience with infidelity and lies.

I could not believe that he was capable of finding another rare jewel such as me, after all that we had experienced together. I assumed that I was the best, the only, and he was totally satisfied with me. I cried and cried. I had never felt like that in my entire life!

What was wrong with me? What did I do to make him want another? How could I change to make him want me and forsake all others? It is so funny how I challenged myself and my rareness to try to keep him.

Of course, I gave him another opportunity to show me how important I was to him and how much he really loved me, but again he failed and I cried. But now, four years later I am finally done. It's a wrap and I must move on with life.

He made a fool of me, my grades began to fall, and that did not make my family happy at all. I had to release myself from the situation. It took me some time to really get over him, but I did it.

I began to really focus on my studies and started to enjoy life and have fun again.

Of course, there were always interested candidates, but I was not ready for a few years. I wanted to cleanse my soul of the impurities that it had incurred from the previous tragedy.

As my college years came near an end, there was another gentleman who was quite interested in me. He was very different and so thoughtful and my father really loved him. In the beginning, we had a great connection.

I wanted to do nothing more but to be in his presence. I was so open and I was addicted to him like an addict needing a fix. I was totally whipped.

Once again, I was truly blind. I now know what they mean when they say 'love is blind.' I would have done anything for him. I ignored all the signs that became so evident in our relationship.

Whatever he wanted to do, whatever he wanted me to do, I was his walking puppet. I experienced some amazing firsts with him.

Despite that, the good did not outweigh the bad. I realized much later why I stayed with him so long. I felt I would never find another guy that could put it down like he had.

I guess it was the thrill of the climaxes and the joy of the pain. He decided I was the one, and we were going to spend our lives together.

A day soon came when I began to feel like he was spending too much time away from me. I could not contact him when I needed or wanted to. He would not return my phone calls.

I knew that there was a problem and I decided I was done, because I had learned from the previous guy how to quit and walk away.

I did not want to continue to feel the way that I did, but I stayed anyway ignoring what was evidently clear. Here I am, again, faced with the reality of infidelity, the difference this time was I decided that I would give him a dose of his own actions.

Why did you want to be with me forever, but choose to be with another? Why did you break the bond that we had? What did I do so wrong that made you change your mind?

I cooked and cleaned and took great care of you. I serviced you in so many ways that I am surprised you had the energy to service someone else.

I did not take the time to reflect on all the great things that my dad instilled in me. My morals and standards were out the window.

My foundation was still there, but it was clouded with disappointments and hurt. I was angry and very vengeful. I was not having it.

I learned from the first guy how to lie and how to get down and dirty with the best of them. I was no fool to the game and about now it was on and popping!

We were playing games and being very foolish. Truly the kind of situations we put ourselves in, someone could have been killed.

I was so cold, and knew just how to make him mad with the stunts I pulled. I knew which buttons to push and I maximized on it every chance I got.

All and all, I was very hurt on the inside. The angrier I became, the more vengeful I acted.

I decided it was really over and I could no longer demean my character and my teachings. As you can imagine, things got really dangerous, so much so my father had me to file a restraining order.

It was time for a change. After six years of emotional ups and downs, it was finally over.

I am now well into my adult life and stumbled across a guy that was 'cool.' We were not planning on being in a relationship, but it just happened and we progressed into an unknown situation with no blueprint.

We both had been in some gruesome relationships, and we were tired of the drama and the emotional roller coasters that we had experienced.

I kept this a secret for a while from my family just in case it did not work. The only person that had some knowledge about my newfound situation was my brother, and he was a bit leery.

He felt that this guy had fallen from the sky and I would be hurt again. This relationship started out so much differently than the others and there were so many components that were factored in. I just put all my cards on the table. I let go of all my hurt in the past.

I figured this was it. I am all in with my poker face. He was a hustler and a worker. I loved that about him. He reminded me so much of my dad. He had a strong tie with his family and could manage a household.

I knew that I was getting old and at some point I needed to prepare myself for the ultimate and for real this time.

I got close before, but I was hoping that this would be the one, and I would not have to go through anymore horror stories with the male gender.

Things progressed and we did become one unit. I was the happiest person on Earth. I was finally and officially off the market. We were the ideal couple. We were the example of real love and how to enjoy life with that special someone. In addition to his two bundles of joy that were in our care, we welcomed a beautiful son into existence.

I was so thrilled and excited, my first child. God is so great and life was truly amazing. Life has its beautiful moments that make you feel like you are living in a fairytale world, but reality has a way of slapping you and opening your eyes.

I thought that I had seen the last days of being hurt. After experiencing so many days of pure happiness and completeness, I knew there was nothing that could come between the bonds that was created by God ... then I was faced with the most devastating encounter in my life.

My husband, the love of my life, the one that I vowed to spend forever with, has now committed the unthinkable. Here we go again. My heart and my stomach dropped to my feet.

I was literally sick for days. I could not eat, talk, sleep or work. This was a moment of disbelief, anger and overwhelming sadness. All of these emotions were flooding my mind in a matter of seconds over and over again.

I began to lose hair, weight and confidence. I gave him my life, my word, my everything. I was there when he was at his lowest.

I made sacrifices that no other woman would have been willing to do. I put myself last and you first. He was my all in all. I had forsaken all others. Why? How? What is wrong with me?

Every time I love someone, they hurt me. Why? Am I too dark or too light? Is my hair not long enough? Do I need to lose or gain weight? Am I fashionable enough? Should I wear more makeup?

Please tell me what I did that was so bad? I will change for you? Just tell me, please, what I did to make you want another?

To add insult to injury, the other choice was one that I could not believe.

He chose a blue-eyed devil over his Queen that made his life easier and supported him when the chips were down.

I know there is something wrong with me. I thought you said that you loved the curves in my hips and my thighs, yet she has none. You said that you loved the way I danced and how I take over the room when I enter, yet she has no rhythm. You said that you loved how beautiful I am, yet she is very hard on the eyes! She is the complete opposite of what you love about me, so what is it?

My foundation was not in existence. I am low and insecure. I am not worthy of anything. I will never be loved. I will never know what it feels like to be truly happy. I am just here to help others and get nothing in return.

Why? I was honest; I gave you my all, why? You do not love me, you do not want me. I need to really get over this or try to make it work. It was very hard and a major struggle to figure out what I was doing on the earth.

What was my purpose?

It was not until two years after this occurrence that I literally came back to life. I prayed and God gave me the strength I needed to dust myself off and realize what I had been taught all those years growing up.

I did not do anything wrong! I am beautiful and smart. I am worth all the good and more that come to me. I do not need to change anything about me. I am a rare and timeless jewel that was placed in the wrong hands.

People come across commonalities all the time and treat them as such, but rarities should be handled differently. Without the proper training and upbringing, you will misuse a jewel that should be handled with care.

It is not until the jewel has been removed that you realize how you wish you could get another opportunity to appreciate the beauty it possesses.

I am strong and I made it through every infraction on my foundation and it still stands strong. I am a woman with true S.W.A.G (Sister with Astonishing Grace).

All of you were very fortunate to say that you had come in contact with something so beautiful. You were fools to abuse the gift that you received. You will never find one so pure and untarnished. You will go to your grave holding the jewel as the example of what an amazing woman is, a worthy woman, a woman who has talents beyond the norm. You will hold your daughters and sons responsible for exhibiting the greatness that you never knew until you met me. I am worthy of being uttered from your lips of regret for how I was treated.

I am worthy of being discussed at family gatherings as to how I am missed and I was the one. I am worthy of my pictures being on the wall even though you have moved on to another and we are no longer. I am worthy of your other loves being intimidated [by my presence] when we encounter each other in a public place after so many years.

I am worthy of the smiles that come across your face when you envision my beauty. I am worthy of the moment you take to close your eyes and vividly imagine the scent of my body overtaking the room.

I am worthy of the times when you bite your lip thinking about the curves and stride of my step. I am worthy of the vessel that expands from the rush of the blood as you take the time to reminisce about how I could bring tears of joy and uncontrollable shakes.

You know what I am worth, but it really does not matter because I know what I am worth. No one on this earth can and never will make me lose sight of my worthiness again.

I am a woman of worth.

I am worth more than you could ever provide. I just decided to give you an opportunity to experience rarity. I am worth more than the energy you put into pleasing me sexually. I am worth more than the sacrifices you think you have made for me.

Why do I feel this way, because God saw fit to take a part of you to make me because you could not do it alone?

I am here as a gift from God. I owe Him all, not you. He created me and I dare not allow a man who needs help to make me feel worthless. If you were given your rib back, I wonder what the world would be like. Appreciate the gift that was given.

I am worth more than you will ever understand.

I am more than a rib.

Deonna Benton

The ultimate measure of a society is not where we stand in moments of comfort, but where we stand in times of challenge and controversy.

When problems come up, how do we react? Do you look for blame, or do you try to repair it? Am I my sister's keeper? Do we throw up our hands and look for an easier way, or do we learn, adapt and keep pushing?

There is a lot of talk nowadays about 'personal responsibility.' That is great. But it is usually brought up only in finding fault. To show 'responsibility' is to own up to your role in the problem's cause.

We do not often hear about the other side of responsibility – that is, an obligation to be part of the solution. Even when a hardship is not your fault at all, you can – and should – do what you can to fix it. Your skills and abilities create an obligation that only your character can fulfill.

There is a concept that makes a woman special and makes her strong. It dwells deep in her soul and when she feels that she can no longer go forward, it churns, toils and grinds its way through until it is revealed. What is this fire that lives within and sometimes I fail to utilize it or I forget it is the very essence of my being and existence? I am a woman of commitment and I am committed to life and to every involvement and evolvement that surrounds me. How do I commit? What is commitment? When is it the right time to be committed? I don't want to have such a burning fire dwelling within and it is useless. I want to apply this concept to my life and change lives. Am I capable of being committed and displaying commitment?

As life goes on day by day, we encounter so many tasks, obstacles and journeys and are faced with decisions that affect our future, whether negative or positive. As they come in our direction, we must make a decision to tackle them head on and show no fear in the unknown outcomes. Lives always presents stumbling blocks when you think everything is going in your favor; but just know that the commitment you have on the inside will carry you through to see the end of each dilemma and life test. Don't be afraid of your own strengths. Find the confidence in yourself that we seem to always look for from those that surround us, and handle your road blocks with style and grace.

Commitment is passion. We always put forth the effort when we are passionate about certain situations. Normally we choose to be passionate about situations that we can control or that don't cause us any heartache and pain. If life were all about great memories and wonderful days, we would never know our strengths and we would never become better vessels. Pain, hard work, disappointment, over-extending and sacrifice are necessary. In order to be completely committed to our life and all that it encompasses, we must accept that there will be some days that we are uplifted and everything is in order, and there will be days that are gloomy and rough. But commitment will take you through those days and, when the light at the end of the tunnel appears, you can get excited about how you made it through. Be committed to everything no matter the outcome or struggle that it takes to survive. Remember that commitment is your strength.

Commitment is an ongoing life skill that should be displayed daily. We should be committed to our families, our jobs, and beliefs in higher beings. We won't always feel appreciated when we put forth efforts and stay committed to all of these aspects. If we constantly look for gratification from those that we pour into daily, we may end up with mounds of disappointments. Be proud of yourself and understand that no matter if you never get a thank you from your partner, boss, children, family member or friends, you have given your very best and you are appreciated. The gratification from others will come soon enough, but when we constantly look for it we grow impatient and disappointed that we aren't flowered with praise. Be committed to being the first to lend a hand and offer your expertise even if you are not compensated for it. Be the first to over-extend yourself beyond normalcy for someone in need who will never be able to repay you. Be the first to come to the aid of someone who hasn't been very nice to you. That's your gratification. You will feel great about yourself and you will rest well at night knowing that you have sown great deeds into the lives of others – and you will reap a harvest of great deeds.

Commitment is everything that is within you. You are a woman of strength and sacrifice. You are dedicated to every aspect of your life and you tackle all obstacles with the same commitment that you would on a day of no stumbling blocks. You don't waver with what you choose to be committed to. You understand that life is what you make it and you want it to be worth everything so you commit. No matter if you are all alone in problem-solving, you commit. If you have to cry your way to the end, you commit. If your children, husband or family disappoint you, you continue to stay committed to your duties. If no one ever acknowledges how awesome you are and how much value you add to this Earth, you stay committed. It doesn't matter what the outcome appears to be, stay committed. Trouble, pain, heartache, struggle, sleepless nights, long work days and economic hardships only last for a season. Ride the wave to shore and pat yourself on the back because you stayed committed and pushed through every situation to the finish. No need to complain and waste time wishing and whining. Stick your chest out, put a pep in your step, hold your head up and commit to life!

Deonna Benton

Womanhood is defined worth, a tear cried, a promise kept, a lesson passed and a breath taken away to create a path for those who are lost.

Proverbs 31 Woman Infinity and Beyond

"A Culmination of 9 Pillars"

There is a vision of a Godly Woman (that know the world) when we dissect this ageless biblical context of womanhood. We do not find the pigeon-held housewife consumed with diapers, dishes, washing and folding. Nor do we find that her day is controlled by the needs of her family. On the other hand, we do not find that she has tunnel vision and is selfish in her endeavors, leaving her family to survive without her presence.

What we discover is a magnificent, distinguished, diverse, compassionate being who is comfortable and unique in her own skin. This woman has bountiful resources to manage, men, women, livestock and land. She is equally yoked and a true mate. Her mate has respect and confidence in her ability to manage their resources.

She possesses the shrewdness to make the deal in the market, along with the empathy to realize and facilitate the needs of the have-nots. She looks forward to living another day to give of herself. Her family loves her because she is every woman and she is selfless.

In all that she does she finds God first. Her devotion and priority is to serve His will. God's will is her life. She is the manifestation of God on earth. She is a past example for women to use as a current model of excellence.

This woman is strategic in her decisions because she plans and prepares for the future. She is nowhere near knee jerk for a mission and vision is always on her mind.

She masters her life by educating herself. She is worldly and knowledgeable of her surroundings and the surroundings of others.

She is a pillar in her house and in her community. She is effective at home and gives back to the community by carrying herself with dignity and respect while treating others as she carries herself.

She is steadfast in her desire for better things for everyone around her.

She realizes that someone will have the audacity to pass the bar if she consistently sets the bar and the standard high enough. She realizes someone will get it. She is up while others sleep, she prays while others weep.

She is the epitome of commitment and determination. She considers the challenges and opportunities in her path and carefully scrutinizes the state of affairs before making a decision.

She takes pride in her worth and everything that her worth represents.

She is a hard worker and knows the value of teamwork. She delegates with the wisdom of a seasoned manager and the work ethic of subordinates trying to impress. Her thought process is nonjudgmental and relies on facts and figures. She also has mastered the balancing of facts and figures with reason and second chances. She always has a contingency plan but plans so efficiently that the use of it is rare. It must be the weather or something out of her control that she still manages to fix with prayer.

She is versatile in her talents and growth is always in her grasp. Forever trying to be a better example is her task. She knows the power in the tongue as she appreciates brains over bronze.

She is treasured so much in the community that she brings respect to her family's name. She is a mother. She is a father. She is a light in the dark. She is warmth in the cold. She is a way out of no way. She is a God-fearing woman. She is resilience. She is empowered enough to know her weakness. She is enough to know your weakness and not use it against you to tear you down but instead enlighten your ignorance of it to make you better. She realizes that the better she is, the better you will be – and the better you are, the easier it is for her. She believes in collective success. She is hope. She is life. She is a combination of destined souls.

She is a capable combination of all a woman should desire to be.

She is one who knows and minds her business, stays gossip and drama free, and carries herself in a relatable and heartfelt manner that can penetrate the darkest soul or inspire the uninspired. She is God's second gift to the world. She is woman.

Some women are goal driven and list marriage on the low end of priorities scale, while others look to balance marriage, family, and career. A Proverbs 31 woman is about a strong woman. She does not ask for it, yet her actions demand appreciation. You are no different than her. Your life is what you make it. Please know that there is no requirement to be a Proverbs 31 woman. **There is, however, a requirement to those you love and a commitment to yourself to be the best woman you can be.**

About the Authors

Rick Chaffold is the founder of *More Than A Rib*, a movement to advance a deeper and growing appreciation for women by changing how women are portrayed and how women portray themselves. Rick's personal motivation comes from being raised in a drug-filled environment layered with domestic violence. Rick is also a proud father of two teenage daughters where he is not the primary parent. He saw the opportunity to share this message of *More Than A Rib* not only as a way to empower mothers, but also as a way to lead by example and give his daughters some encouraging structure in the midst of challenges that young women face.

Rick has been a motivational teacher and speaker for a diverse range of teen and adult at risk males and females. His diverse employment history has lead him down the service corridor. His history includes Marine Corps, Peace and Correctional Officer in the state of Louisiana, Junior Correctional Officer with the state of Texas and CPS youth counselor with the city of Houston.

A wartime veteran, Rick is currently serving a dynamic role at The Department of Veteran Affairs. Rick's current role is veteran advocate to a diverse group of . Rick's education includes a Bachelors of Science degree in Management and a Master's degree in Business with a concentration in Healthcare. He currently serves as CEO of The ARN Group, a nonprofit that houses companies *More Than A Rib* and *After 5 Event Planning Services*. Rick is consistently motivating and providing public assistance to veterans through Veteran Affairs outreach programs. Rick is also working, producing, and speaking at the More Than A Rib Health Series Forums. Rick travels abroad and is available to speak at your event or to your organization upon request. Rick's topics of expertise are Healthy Relationships (Love yourself 1st), Self Esteem (You are what you Digest), Perspective (Glass Half Empty Glass Half Full 2015 Rule), Increased Production in the Workplace (Empowerment is the Key), Mind Frame (Change it or Die), and Proper Planning Prevents Pitiful Performance (Put it on Paper). Rick can also tailor a presentation to fit your desired subject matter.

For speaking engagements contact

713-320-6856

Varion "Se7en the Poet" Howard originates from Houston's Southside. Se7en's prominent and prolific voice has established this gifted entertainer as the industry's premier inspirational artist. Se7en – Houston's motivational diamond in the rough – is a graduate of Prairie View A&M University, with undergraduate dual degrees in Psychology and Social Work and a Master's degree in Counseling. Se7en's phenomenal and motivational talent has taken the world by storm. "I didn't choose to inspire," he explains. "Inspiration chose me."

Pushing the edge of social consciousness and encouraging all to be true to self is Se7en's purpose. He is vernacularly enticing with prose perfectly pitched to the voice, mentalities, and actions of today's society. Se7en has the ability to connect with the core of your soul and make you laugh, cry, and question life. This ability truly makes him a rare jewel. He is a poet, motivational speaker, author, and host of the longest-running speak easy forums in Houston, Texas. His versatility, humility, and fierce stage presence allows him to speak on life as it evolves.

Se7en's groundbreaking debut album entitled "Make Me Laugh, Make Me Cry" (2005) solidified his standing as a powerhouse in the poetry and motivational speaking arenas. He has since released The White, The Blue Album, and DVD Live from St Johns (all available on iTunes). He is currently working on The Brown Album. Se7en's infectious stage presence coupled with his intellect has positioned him to change the way people experience poetry. "My goal is to bring poetry to the forefront of entertainment. I want people to recognize poetry as a genre of entertainment that not only stands alone, but stands the test of time."

Seven has had the pleasure of working with and motivating such entities as the National Alliance of Black Educators, Black Educator Association (Canada), Chase Bank, Black Academy of Arts and Letters, NAACP, Windsor Village Church, St Johns Church

Downtown, and recently TV Ones Verses and Flow. Varion also speaks at the More Than A Rib Health Series Forums. Varion travels abroad and is available to speak at your event or to your organization upon request. Varion's topics of expertise are diverse ranging from the motivation and guidance of educators and students to the motivation and guidance of executive professionals. Topic include: Productivity, Putting your best Foot Forward (Motivating the Man in the Mirror), The Reinvention of ME (Recharge, Restructure, Reinvent), and The Necessities of Change (Flexibility = Growth).

For speaking engagements contact

713-320-6856

Coming Soon

More Than A Rib Presents:
The Rib "The Man's Right of Passage to Becoming a Man"

Two Ears One Mouth
The Art to Communicating with Men

Egos vs. Child Welfare: The Joint Parenting Journey

More Than a Rib Presents:
From the Street to the Concrete Men and Their Emotions

www.ingramcontent.com/pod-product-compliance
Lightning Source LLC
Chambersburg PA
CBHW060003100426
42740CB00010B/1381

* 9 7 8 0 5 7 8 1 2 5 9 7 8 *